BRANDING

A BRAND IS JUST A LOGO
AND OTHER POPULAR MISCONCEPTIONS

Simon Bailey
Andy Milligan

KoganPage

First published in Great Britain and the United States in 2019 by Kogan Page Limited

2nd Floor, 45 Gee Street	c/o Martin P Hill Consulting	4737/23 Ansari Road
London	122 W 27th Street	Daryaganj
EC1V 3RS	New York, NY 10001	New Delhi 110002
United Kingdom	USA	India

© Simon Bailey and Andy Milligan 2019

ISBNs

Hardback	978 0 7494 9771 2
Paperback	978 0 7494 8309 8
Ebook	978 0 7494 8310 4

British Library Cataloguing-in-Publication Data

A CIP record for this book is available from the British Library.

Library of Congress Cataloging-in-Publication Data

A CIP record is available for this title from the Library of Congress.

Typeset by Integra Software Services, Pondicherry
Print production managed by Jellyfish
Printed and bound in Great Britain by CPI Group (UK) Ltd, Croydon CR0 4YY

To Dad, KP and Caffeine.
Simply the best.

SIMON

CONTENTS

ABOUT THE AUTHORS

Simon and Andy have known each other for over twenty years. Much of that time has been spent working around the world helping impatient business leaders deliver brand-led growth. Simon has led several well-known branding consultancies and Andy is co-founder of The Caffeine Partnership. Both appear regularly in the media, writing and commentating on brands. Andy has also published a number of other books on branding and delivering a branded customer experience, including *Bold* and *On Purpose*.

PREFACE

There are many books on branding and there are many theories and approaches to the subject of branding. In the end, though, most of these are essentially the same and all come to similar conclusions about the importance of branding and the key principles that underpin successful brands. All agree that brands are important assets for businesses, that consumers value them, and that underpinning them are essential rules of consistency, clarity, relevance and differentiation.

However, despite the fact that there is so much agreement on the value and the meaning of brands, there are still many myths that abide about the precise role, nature and worth of brands. Probably these myths persist for two reasons. One is that, although the discipline of branding is well established, it is not such a formalized practice nor an integral legal part of corporate governance that its rules and standards have been set down, agreed upon and instituted in regulatory bodies around the world. So there is an understandable degree of variation about the way in which branding is interpreted and practised. Two, the nature of branding compared to, say, accounting and law, is such that it is highly visible and ubiquitous in the lives of all of us. We are all exposed to brands and branding on a daily basis. We consume them, we reject them, and we admire them according to our personal attitudes and daily experiences. This means that almost everyone in the world has an opinion about brands and branding. And some of these opinions are shaped by a few voices in the media who worry about the insidious effect of consumerism upon our society and about the role of profiteering corporations in our world. Some people see brands as the poster child for an exploitative capitalist economy. Naomi Klein probably delivers the best-known articulation of that view.[1]

We, the authors of this book, have spent all of our working lives in the field of brands and branding. We have seen brands that are good, brands that are bad and brands that are largely indifferent and unremarkable. We have always believed that brands are valuable.

Developed and managed properly, they are an economic and social good. They help businesses grow, thus stimulating wealth creation, employment and taxation. And they help people get more quickly the things that they want, value and often need, be it cars or computers, milk or a mortgage, travel or telecommunications. Conversely, it is easier to punish a business by rejecting a brand which fails to perform a useful service or is associated with and owned by a company whose practices are either antisocial or in other ways unethical. Such consumer power can drive changes in corporate practices and thus improvements in the world in which we live. The growing consumer demand for Fairtrade branded products or environmentally sensitive production and packaging processes is evidence of this.

So this book is written from the perspective of many years of experience working with brands and brand owners all around the world and in different sectors. It is written from a place of positive appreciation of what brands can help companies and consumers achieve. Finally, of course, it is written from the perspective of ourselves as consumers of brands, just like everyone else.

Myths of Branding will seek to challenge some received wisdom and also bring the practice of branding up to date. We will seek to debunk some well-established myths – that branding is just about identity, that brands don't have any real value, that brands exist just to drive premium pricing – but we will also look at how technology is really impacting brands, whether brand loyalty really is being diminished, the extent to which the customer is always right, what happens if you lose trust. We will also look at some of the myths that surround the practitioner, for example that brands don't matter in business, that there are no real tools to help you manage your brand, that customers want a conversation with your brand. We will also explore other myths, but hopefully this will give you a feel for what is to come.

This book represents our informed and expert opinions. Nevertheless, they are just that – our opinions. Others may disagree with the conclusions we draw about the myths that we have listed in this book. Others may feel that we have ignored some myths. We would be delighted to hear from anyone who takes a different view to us or thinks there are other myths that need to be challenged or can be proven.

In the end brands are built fundamentally on personal opinion, the opinion of one person deciding that they prefer or like one brand more than another. So it is only right that we encourage people to share and express their opinions on what we think.

We have included a very brief introductory chapter about the nature of brands in general, and the difference between brands and branding. There are so many books, as we have already mentioned, that cover these topics in depth already that for us to write about them here would be superfluous. Instead, throughout the book we have referenced the many books in which these very helpful and useful studies of brands can be found.

However, we have throughout the book explained in the context of the particular myth we are discussing, what brands are, how they work, what their value is, how we as customers or consumers appreciate them, and how companies and indeed individual personalities now manage them. We felt that was a better and more relevant way of addressing those topics.

We have chosen 20 myths that we feel are the most common and persistent ones relating to the subject of brands and branding. Some of these myths have been around for as long as we have been practitioners in this field, which is almost 30 years. Some are more recent and are a result perhaps of the growing importance and thus growing academic and quasi-academic scrutiny to which brands are subjected. With each myth we have attempted to fairly represent why it has come about, as well, of course, as what it is. The majority of each chapter is given over to an exposition of the relevant issues to which the myth relates and for the most part repudiation or occasionally a sympathetic clarification of them.

We did not write this book as a linear narrative, and we don't expect you to read it in that way. We want you to be happy to dip in and out of it. You can choose to read any one or several of the myths that appear to interest you most without reading any others. Or you can read them all in any order you like. If you read all the chapters, you will find certain references or examples reoccur in different chapters, albeit in slightly different ways to support different points.

We have written the book with the general reader in mind, not the marketing professional for whom many of the concepts and examples will be familiar.

For that reason, we have also attempted to keep our language as simple, clear and understandable as possible. In the field of marketing and business generally and in branding specifically, there is too often a desire to use long complicated terms and words for what are already abstract concepts. We'd rather attempt to make what can sometimes be complex issues as easy to understand as possible. As we often say to our colleagues, client and friends, 'Branding is not rocket science. It's way more complicated than that.'

We hope that you will enjoy the book and appreciate it in the spirit that it was written.

Note

1 Naomi Klein, *No Logo*, Vintage, 1999

INTRODUCTION

On myths and brands

According to the Oxford Dictionary a myth is 'A traditional story, especially one concerning the early history of a people or explaining a natural or social phenomenon, and typically involving supernatural beings or events.' In this book we can't promise very much of the supernatural or even an exploration of naturally occurring phenomena, but we can promise that we will examine the stories and received wisdom that surround the subject of brands and branding.

Before we move on it is probably worth asserting the difference between 'brands' and 'branding'. Brands are traditionally seen as a mix of tangible and intangible assets that act as a marker or identifier and, in legal terms, 'separate the undertaking of one business from that of another'. Brands are protectable as trademarks and over the years it has become possible to protect brand names, identities, colours, sounds and even different pack shapes. Harley-Davidson has even managed to legally protect the unique roar of their engines.

Brand owners in turn have sought to vest their assets with a distinctive meaning that helps to build appeal and saliency with their customers – this process of creating and managing brands is often referred to as branding – the uniquely challenging mix that is the art and science of brand building.

Brands and branding

Brands are everywhere. As well as adding colour, interest and fun, they help consumers to make choices. They can act as a welcome shorthand, speeding up decision-making; they can build affinity and meaning and even help some of us build our own personal identity – the heart of the notion that to some extent 'we are what we buy'.

And yet much suspicion surrounds the science and art of brand building, as though in some way it is a dishonest exercise, something designed to deceive and obfuscate, something weighting the scales in favour of the corporation at the expense of the consumer – and that's even before we get to the often touted idea that global brands and the corporations that own them are solely responsible for globalization and the death of the high street.

Brands exist because they are in effect the leitmotifs of the human condition. We like to signal ownership, we like to project meaning onto the things that surround us, we like things that reduce risk and act as a guarantor of quality, we like things that make us feel different and special and we love things that fire our imaginations and leave us entertained and exhilarated.

Brands exist because we do.

How it all began

We will never really be able to accurately pinpoint when the practice of branding began but it seems safe to assume that for as long as people have been producing goods for sale or exchange they have been endorsing them and leaving their mark on them. Brands historically began life as a mark of ownership (for example on livestock) as well as a form of primitive guarantee – attesting to quality and provenance – and over the millennia brands have evolved to become a complex mix of the tangible and intangible.

As late as the 1960s if you had asked UK customers in the high street to talk about their favourite brands, they would probably have referenced a series of consumer brands, for example Heinz, Cadbury's, Hoover and Mars. Brands as we know them were inextricably linked to the post-war boom and closely associated with improving living standards and increasing prosperity. Brands were there principally to simplify choice, and provide a guarantee of quality and provenance. Some brand owners were experimenting with ways of building meaning into their products – most famously VW with their 'Lemon' advertising for the Beetle, but in most instances brands were still acting as identifiers – a name, an identity, a tagline, a jingle.

The rise of the service brand

It wasn't really until the late '70s and early '80s that the concept of brands began to extend into all areas of business. As entities were privatized, markets deregulated and competition became fiercer so the need to differentiate your business became greater. Utilities, telecoms providers, banks, insurance companies and airlines were all now enthusiastically embracing the power of branding. As brand owners fought for space in your mind, advertising became incredibly influential. The focus was on imbuing products and services with meaning so that you as the customer could surround yourself with the brands that best represented you – the very notion of shopping as a form of personal expression. Even businesses serving other businesses began to realize that having a brand was an important business support – even cynics had to attest to the power of the statement 'No one ever got fired for hiring IBM'.

Brands were now seen as more than just a logo or a tagline; they were seen as opportunities to create meaning.

The experience economy

In the 1990s and early 2000s we saw brands extend their meaning to embrace the experience economy. As we accumulated more stuff, so it became more interesting to seek out unique or engaging experiences. Virgin Atlantic helped customers to feel like a rock star, coffee shops offered a 'third space' between work and home, Apple provided an entire digital ecosystem, networks of gyms promised to transform your body and your lifestyle. Brands could now shape or even immerse you in a branded world.

The digital economy

We are now in the middle of a digital revolution, which is still gaining velocity. The ability to instantly find, compare and share information has had a transformative effect on businesses and brands. Today it is increasingly difficult to separate the brand from the business that supports it – they have effectively become one and the same thing. When you can instantly compare price and product attributes, when you can find out who owns a company and how they treat their staff, when you can instantly review and post your comments online, when you can communicate directly with a company via a social media platform, when word of mouth has never been more important, then brands become inextricably linked with how a business behaves.

That is also why customers are no longer just concerned with who you are and what you do; they are also interested in why you do it. The notion of Purpose is becoming increasingly important. Is what you are saying to your staff congruent with what you say to your customers? Are you behaving in a way that is authentic? Do you seek to mitigate the negative impacts that your business may have? Do you operate to a clear set of principles?

As brands have changed so has the practice of branding. What began as naming, graphic design and advertising has morphed into a broader set of activities. If branding began as a way of helping brand owners create clear attribution, it has evolved to encompass an operating system, the process of finding an authentic, distinctive and ownable idea that unites staff and customers and then aligning all aspects of the way the business behaves behind that idea.

Whatever your view on brands and branding, whether you see them as a force for good or the bellwethers of a broken capitalist system, we hope you will find something in this book that will challenge your perspective or your thinking.

It won't surprise you to find out that we are supporters of brands; we see them as an integral part of free expression and free enterprise. They are also increasingly an important way of holding businesses to account. But beyond that, we also see them as intimately connected with what it means to be human.

**MYTH
1**

BRANDS ARE JUST A WAY OF CHARGING YOU MORE FOR THE SAME PRODUCT

*'We' the customers ultimately decide what and how
much we are prepared to pay. People buy brands
for more reasons than just the product.*

One of the most common criticisms levelled at brands is that they are a marketing scam, a way of badging a relatively generic product or service and charging you more money for it. How many times have you heard someone say, 'You're just paying for the branding'?

In fact a brand is rarely just a way of charging you more for the same product, because the product is only part of what people pay for when they buy a brand. It's important to keep in mind that the value of a brand resides in the mind of the consumer. As Jeff Bezos is reputed to have said: 'A brand is what people say about you when you are not in the room.' Identifiers can be owned, brands in their truest form cannot.

Every brand is unique. It's true that some brands are not particularly distinctive and in some cases may not represent good value.

But taken as a whole, two brands operating even in the same category cannot by definition be exactly the same. A brand is the consequence of all of the actions taken to build and sustain it and the subsequent impression this activity forms in the mind of the consumer, for good or bad.

The real reason businesses invest in brand building is because, done well, an effective brand generates demand and (to a varying degree) sustains loyalty. That in turn drives revenue and sustains margin. Good brands also help to reduce risk. A well-established and well-run brand (especially one that has thrived over many decades) stands a good chance of being able to weather volatile economic cycles. In effect it starts with an inbuilt advantage.

Of course, there are plenty of examples of brands seeking to take advantage of consumers but in most instances these brands rarely endure. Gerald Ratner found out to his great cost in the early '90s that consumers don't like to be cynically manipulated; he appeared to effectively destroy his own jewellery brand when he reputedly admitted at a conference that the products in Ratners (and by implication the rest of his group) were 'crap'. After that revelation there was seemingly no way back for Gerald or his eponymous stores, not because he couldn't have addressed the product quality but because overnight the brand appeared to become fatally synonymous with being taken for a sucker. Gerald was fired shortly afterwards.

There will always be attempts to give customers a poor deal, ranging from the fraudulent re-badging of inferior product (counterfeiting) through to the more cynical exploitation of existing brand equity (re-badging) but neither scenario is sustainable in the long term. Even the very best counterfeit goods require you to in effect pay less for less and consumers very quickly get wise to attempts to insult their intelligence.

Brands that seek an unjustified price premium or treat consumers with barefaced contempt don't tend to thrive. And that is the crucial point that undermines this myth.

The truth is that it is 'we', the customers, who ultimately decide what and how much we are prepared to pay.

Marlboro Friday serves to illustrate this point. Back in 1993 Philip Morris decided overnight to cut the price of Marlboro cigarettes by 20 per cent. They had realized that their market share was being eroded by cheaper brands and that they had effectively reached a price ceiling. Many commentators saw this as the 'death of brands' and as a result of the price cut the Philip Morris share price fell by 26 per cent. Other consumer brands were similarly affected. Of course, this didn't presage the end of premium pricing. Philip Morris continued to invest heavily in all aspects of brand building. But it did demonstrate that it is customers who ultimately determine what they are prepared to pay.

We are paying for psychological fulfilment and not product satisfaction

The notion of what supports a price premium is probably not as straightforward as it first appears. In many instances a price premium can be sustained over a competitor in spite of the fact that within a specific category, product or service quality is in fact highly comparable. As long as a product or service meets an acceptable quality threshold a consumer may well be prepared to pay more for the brand that they perceive as either higher quality or simply more distinctive or appealing. Customers are prepared to pay more for a product that they perceive as genuinely different or distinctive.

Let's apply this thinking to a specific category. A consumer looking for a high-end luxury handbag or piece of statement luggage is unlikely to have the depth of knowledge to be able to really scrutinize the intrinsic quality of the products they are considering. Will they really know how to appraise the quality of the leather and the stitching? Will they be familiar with the different production methods or the techniques deployed by individual artisans? Do they know what facets will guarantee durability and longevity? The answer to most of these questions is likely to be objectively 'no'. What matters is that the product meets a quality threshold that can (prima facie) support the price premium; the actual choice is likely to be made around a combination of colour, design and branded preference. In relation to the points made earlier, it is also worth reflecting on the fact that both the design of the bag and the brand itself will have required considerable investment. These are the elements that drive demand in this category: the uniqueness of the design, the relative scarcity of the bag, the quality of the advertising, the careful celebrity endorsement and subsequent social media campaign, the hard-fought editorial endorsement, the retail (in store or online) experience and even the quality of the packaging. Buying a statement bag is about aligning yourself with a very specific set of branded associations. You are buying a psychological or emotional benefit more than a product. You are buying an affirmation of your self-worth or identity.

Exactly the same happens in the automotive market which, as it is based on engineering, you might have thought would involve highly rational purchase decisions. It would seem reasonable to suppose that the quality, reliability and durability of cars increase broadly in line with their price. The more expensive or premium the car, the higher the quality; in this context you would also expect the less reliable car brands to be struggling to sell their cars. In fact it turns out not to be like this at all. Because quality and reliability have improved so much across the whole category, this no longer has the direct bearing you would expect. Premium manufacturers such as BMW, Mercedes and Land Rover often lag significantly behind their mid-market Asian counterparts in reliability, but this has no real observable impact on their overall sales success. The category is heavily influenced by design, performance, price and above all image.

We all have different levels of price sensitivity

Different sets of customers will also tend to value different things. While one customer might baulk at the idea of paying Apple a thousand pounds for the privilege of buying their latest mobile handset, another will queue up all night outside a store to do just that. It will all depend on what the customer considers important. If the customer values an intuitive interface, seamless connectivity, elegant design and the kudos that goes with owning the latest generation of smart technology, they are likely to perceive Apple's pricing as justified; contrast this with a customer who cares less about interface design and instead values the freedom, flexibility and lower prices afforded by one of the alternative device manufacturers. For this customer Apple will look immediately less enticing and quite possibly very expensive.

A recent survey by Deloitte referenced in an article by Kantar Millward Brown demonstrated that not all customers have the same level of price sensitivity. For example, 32 per cent of respondents in the Deloitte survey comprised a group called 'affluent convenience shoppers', and this group tended to be the most brand loyal and the least price sensitive.

How important your category is to people will determine how generally price sensitive they are, but in any category different types of customer will exhibit different levels of price sensitivity.

Apple's pricing enables them to invest considerable sums in innovation and design but conversely it also reassures their customers that they are buying genuine quality. The same applies in other categories. Stella Artois was able to charge a premium price for its lager because it invested a lot of money in making its brand appear aspirational; this same approach worked for the Mexican beer Dos Equis. It appears we are often reassured by the 'reassuringly expensive'.

Price premium is sustained when there is a constant justification

The idea that brands are just a way of charging you more for the same product might hold more credence in instances where the role of the brand plays a much less significant role in the decision to purchase. You might expect to find this in categories that are regarded to a greater or lesser extent as commoditized. For example, fuel retailing. While you may have a preferred 'place' where you fill up your car or buy your oil, it is likely that this preference is as much driven by location as it is by brand. It is very difficult for the average driver to assess the relative performance of different brands of fuel – the engine is either working or it isn't – this all helps support the notion that all fuel is essentially the same and that the big distributors (branded suppliers) are effectively colluding to keep the price of a commodity product higher than it needs to be.

Eventually the supermarket chains spotted this and so they decided to stop retailing branded fuels BP, Esso etc. In the late 1980s when they started to retail own-branded fuels (Tesco, Sainsbury's etc), you could fill up during your weekly shop and pay less for your fuel than you would with a branded supplier. Except of course it wasn't as simple as that. While the big branded suppliers could control and guarantee the quality of their fuels, the same could not be said for the supermarkets. The supermarkets were buying fuels from a variety of suppliers and specifying a minimum performance standard. This in turn led to a number of instances where the supermarkets unwittingly sold customers poor-quality low-grade fuels, which were found to be negatively impacting engine performance and in some instances even causing permanent damage to customers' vehicles. In early 2007 *Autocar* magazine reported thousands of customers being impacted by poor-grade fuel being dispensed at Tesco and Morrisons stations. The problem was reported as having been traced to a single terminal in Essex. Of course, these issues were sorted out and problems rectified, but a seed of doubt had been planted. A few pence a litre extra might actually be worth the investment, especially if you are someone who cares about their car or have chosen to run a high-performance vehicle.

The branded suppliers have not just rested on their laurels either. They have continued to invest heavily in new fuel additives and derivatives. They launched fuels that could look after your engine and improve fuel economy. Yes, the benefits might be marginal and hard to see, but they could at least be substantiated by science.

They could also offer premium-grade fuels along with the implicit guarantee that in buying from a branded supplier you are doing the very best for your vehicle. And it didn't stop there. Perhaps with half an eye on the future the branded suppliers and their franchise holders began investing in the retail experience: you don't mind paying a bit more for your fuel if you can have the convenience of picking up a few groceries and a decent cup of coffee at the same time.

So even in an apparently commoditized category like fuel retailing, a potent mix of ingenuity and competition has ensured that no two fuels are quite the same.

We are often prepared to pay for difference

Even when a brand looks or feels similar to a competitor, you can often be paying more because a brand has chosen to behave differently. One of the things often overlooked is that the very big brands are often held to a higher level of scrutiny than less well-known ones. They become in effect the category standard bearers. When you buy a pair of Nike trainers, you are paying for the investment in design, materials, image and sponsorship, but you are also paying for the investment in the supply chain. To continue building its business, Nike has had to face up to some of its broader social responsibilities. It has had to regulate suppliers, ensure that contractors adhere to specific conditions and pay workers fairly. Global brands know that they have to factor good behaviour into their business model, because it is increasingly (and rightly) expected by their customers. Nike also know that they are coveted by some customers who struggle to afford their products; that's why they are investing in local communities. They cannot afford to take their customers for granted, and nor should they.

As technology has made it much easier for rivals to copy a product or service advantage, so brands have increasingly sought to differentiate themselves through the power of experiences. Brands that offer memorable or distinctive branded experiences stand out and get talked about. It is much harder for a competitor to replicate a unique brand experience, especially one driven by the individual culture of a competitor organization. Virgin Atlantic, Metro Bank, giffgaff, Starbucks, Apple and Amazon are just a few examples of businesses that have sought to build competitive advantage in this way. By understanding what their customers really value, these businesses have been able to develop a few highly distinctive hallmarks that collectively add up to a unique branded experience. By making discrete and purposeful choices they have (in many cases) been able to not only build powerful brands but also maintain price competitiveness.

It is true that some businesses will offer the same product for sale under more than one brand name, but very rarely in the same country or territory. Automotive manufacturers, for example, will occasionally re-badge a car for a different country or region, but this is usually connected to a specific market context such as a brand acquired as the result of a larger acquisition. It is rarely an attempt to deceive.

In brands we trust

There is one category of product, however, where – at least prima facie – brands are routinely used to charge you more for the same (or at least very similar) product. Pharmaceuticals. When a drug is initially licensed, the business that developed that drug is granted a patent for a fixed period. This arrangement (depending on the type of drug) allows the company to commercially market the drug (free for a period from direct competition), recoup their investment in research and development and make a profit. Eventually, however, the patent expires and competitors make other generic versions of the drug. This arrangement is much in evidence with over-the-counter medicines. Take ibuprofen (a non-steroidal anti-inflammatory). It began life back in the UK in 1969 as a prescription-only drug, but was later licensed and incorporated into a number of well-known over-the-counter brands, one of the best known being Nurofen, now a billion-dollar brand. But eventually ibuprofen became accessible to generic manufacturers and this has resulted in the situation we have today where, depending on who you buy it from, you can pay up to three times more for the same drug.

Of course, it can also be argued that some consumers understand this trade-off; perhaps it is the price we choose to pay to ensure that the pharmaceutical companies keep investing in research and development? Additionally, many of the branded drugs contain additional ingredients to help them improve their overall action and efficacy and, to return to the point made earlier in this chapter, when you buy the leading pharmaceutical brand you are also buying peace of mind; a guarantee of quality and efficacy, which in a category where up to 50 per cent of a drug's effectiveness can be directly attributed to the placebo effect, really matters.

Ultimately then it is the customers that decide what price they are prepared to pay for a brand. Rather than being fooled into parting with more money than we need to, we often actively collude with companies to pay a premium, often because we are buying into so much more than just a simple product or service.

Further reading

Ben Goldacre, *Bad Science*, HarperCollins Publishers, 2009

Kantar Millward Brown, How smart brands command a price premium, www.millwardbrown.com/Insights/Point-of-View/How_Smart_ Brands_Command_a_Premium_Price/default.aspx

Alvin J Silk and Bruce Isaacson, Philip Morris: Marlboro Friday (A). Harvard Business School Case 596-001, September 1995 (Revised December 1997)

ONCE LOST, TRUST CAN NEVER BE REBUILT

If you have a strong brand and a desire to take restorative action, trust can often be either fully or at least partially restored.

Brands, just like people, can get things wrong. Most of the time these mistakes are innocent enough, small everyday errors impacting a small number of customers, the usual stuff of business, unfortunate and frustrating for the customer but relatively straightforward to rectify and resolve to the customer's satisfaction. But occasionally things can go very badly wrong. These are mistakes that are so large and so systemic that they have the potential to jeopardize the future existence of the brand and the undertaking that supports it.

What tends to sit behind these kinds of mistakes is bad behaviour (in all its various forms) and the reason these mistakes are so damaging is that they directly impact upon trust. If your customers don't believe you are trustworthy the consequences can be dramatic.

So if trust is hard won and easily lost, can it really be rebuilt? And if it is true that some brands have disappeared completely as a result of their behaviour, why is it that some brands are seemingly able to recover from a breach of trust while others never recover?

Well, here's the good news (especially if you are in the middle of a major issue): it is usually possible to rebuild trust, but first you need to understand both the nature of the breach and the actions required to address the problem.

Intentional, negligent or in open contempt?

The single biggest determinant that dictates the outcome of these types of event is the nature of the breach that has occurred. Was the breach intentional or 'merely' negligent? Was the breach the result of a direct instruction from the top of the organization or a rogue employee? Is the breach the result of a fundamental disregard or even an open contempt for customers? It also helps if you have deep reserves of cash and a large amount of existing goodwill.

At the beginning of the book, we touched upon Gerald Ratner and the subsequent collapse of his brand. His highly successful brand folded in the early '90s amid a media storm after he spoke at a conference and openly admitted (with considerable hubris) that his own products were 'crap'. This admission was fatal for the brand because it showed an open contempt both for his product and more importantly for his own customers. No one likes to be taken for a sucker, especially when it concerns items that are frequently bought as expressions of love or endearment. Ratner's brand was fatally holed below the waterline.

Deepwater Horizon

Contrast that with the BP Deepwater Horizon scandal, which began on 20 April 2010. It seems reasonable to suppose that no one at BP intentionally set out to cause an environmental disaster, but Deepwater finished up being the largest accidental oil spill in the history of the petroleum industry. A sea floor gusher flowed for 87 days unchecked and subsequently discharged an estimated 4.9 million barrels of oil into the Gulf of Mexico. Eleven people lost their lives and some of these were never found. Operators Transocean and Halliburton were also implicated in the scandal and BP was eventually found to be grossly negligent. Yet in spite of criticism of leadership at the time and the potential damage to BP's fledgling green credentials (remember 'Beyond Petroleum'?) BP is still very much with us.

The key point here is that there was no intentionality to this disaster. Although BP was found grossly negligent and arguably should have foreseen the potential for an accident, it was in the end just that, a terrible accident. Most people appreciate that oil exploration is a dirty, dangerous and (at least for now) a necessary activity. Oil is increasingly difficult to find and increasingly difficult to extract. Yes, there were clearly failings and there may have been systemic issues at play but no one at BP 'intended' for the leak to occur. There is no doubt, though, that a less well capitalized and strategically important business might not have managed to survive. BP also made a well-documented hash of its early attempt to manage the situation and this ultimately resulted in the departure of its Chief Executive, Tony Hayward. The total cost to BP of the Deepwater Horizon disaster is currently estimated at around $65bn. The complexity of the accident and its contributory causes, together with BP's ability to be able to pay huge reparations, has helped to ensure the brand's survival. But the environmental impact is still being felt today: trust is slowly being rebuilt, but among certain constituencies this is likely to take a lifetime.

Dieselgate

The more recent VW 'Dieselgate' scandal serves to illustrate a number of important points. For those not acquainted with the detail of this story, VW was found to have secretly fitted 'defeat' devices to over 500,000 diesel cars sold in the US. The purpose of this device was to ensure that under certain test conditions the car would emit less pollution than it would under normal 'real world' driving conditions. This allowed the cars to appear to pass the stringent US emissions tests when in fact they were in normal conditions exceeding the specified limit. The car was actually able to detect when it was being tested and the device would be automatically activated for the duration of the test. In this instance there was clearly an intention to deceive both the customer and the regulator and it caused global shockwaves across the automotive sector. It was particularly shocking because VW was (until this point) very highly regarded and regularly posted the highest trust scores of any mainstream manufacturer.

For a short while it looked as though this crisis had the propensity to destroy VW, but eventually things began to stabilize. VW was probably helped by a number of factors. While this was clearly a big issue and there had been an obvious intention to deceive, the impact appeared (at least initially) to be limited to a specific number of cars in a specific territory. VW, prior to the scandal, was regarded as a global powerhouse, producing safe and reliable cars and while not good for VW's reputation the scandal did not fatally undermine VW's reputation for engineering competency and excellence. They were further helped by the lack of an apparent link (no direct instruction) between senior management and a global testing regime that could at best be described as highly flawed. Trust in VW had been severely damaged (the business posted its worst-ever financial performance in 80 years,) but the business has managed to regroup. Again, just like BP, the resignation of the Chief Executive helped draw some of the fire but deep pockets have also helped. The scandal is estimated by UBS to have cost VW in the region of $42bn. Since the scandal VW has worked extremely hard at rebuilding trust and while the scandal initially impacted sales, in 2017 they became the world's largest car company. Their share price is also improving, albeit more slowly; at July 2018, VW was trading at approximately €143 per share. That is down from its 2015 high of €240 but up from €136 in 2016.

What BP and VW both demonstrate is that brands can survive catastrophic events but much depends on the strength of the brand before the crisis as well as the nature of the breach – how and in what way has trust been impacted? That is not the end of the story, though; assuming you have a survivable event, how do you start the process of rebuilding trust?

Righting the wrongs

Between 2006 and 2009 a number of customers started reporting incidents of 'unintended acceleration' across a range of Toyota and Lexus models (Toyota's premium brand). Around the same time a number of Toyota drivers were involved in fatal accidents and these were directly attributed by the US National Highway Traffic Safety Administration (NHTSA) to episodes of unintended acceleration as a consequence of a defective accelerator unit. This had the potential to have a catastrophic impact on one of the world's largest carmakers, especially one that had built its worldwide reputation on the reliability and durability of its vehicles. Once Toyota realized the seriousness of the situation, however, they quickly took decisive action. They finished up recalling and rectifying over nine million vehicles, initially to replace defective floor mats (first believed to be the source of the issue) and later to replace defective accelerators. Defective software was also later identified as an issue in wireless accelerators. The total cost of the recall was estimated at $5bn but both the willingness to address the issue and the scale of the recall helped to reassure customers. This incident demonstrated what could be achieved when a brand was prepared to take ownership and get proactive.

Samsung did something similar when their customers started reporting that significant numbers of their latest mobile device, the

Galaxy Note 7, were catching fire and in some cases even exploding. For a premium global brand increasingly synonymous with cutting-edge mobile technology this had the potential to cause significant damage to Samsung's reputation and undermine customers' trust in their brand. Once the brand realized the extent of the problem, as well as the risk that the device could explode, the business took unprecedented action. Initially Samsung recalled 2.5 million devices and swapped them for devices with different batteries, believing wrongly that this would rectify the issue. When it didn't (one of the replacement phones allegedly caught fire on a plane while it was switched off) Samsung then recalled all of the Note 7s and even took the unusual step of 'bricking' (effectively disabling) any devices still in circulation so that they could no longer be used. By admitting the issue, performing extensive testing and then being unrelenting in their quest to resolve the issue, Samsung were able to quickly recover and move on. Customers largely kept faith with Samsung and the brand continues to go from strength to strength.

Whether the issue at hand is a major crisis or even just an embarrassing incident, the extent to which trust is impacted is dependent on a) the strength of the brand before the incident b) the nature of the breach and c) how the brand chooses to react.

Samsung took a decision to act quickly in the interest of their customers. They made a mistake, apologized, took clear steps to resolve the issue and then implemented in a way that was consistent with their brand, including being prepared to face up to the full financial impact of their mistake. This contrasts with BP and VW, both of whom appeared to take longer to realize both the seriousness and culpability of their respective situations. Perhaps their relative size and organizational structure impeded their ability to act in a more agile manner? Eventually, however, these brands did grasp the seriousness of the situation and faced up to their responsibilities.

So evidently trust can be rebuilt (or at least partially restored) but how a brand chooses to act has a big impact on the eventual outcome. Even when a breach is much less serious, the same playbook still applies. Technology and social media have the power to amplify any small transgression. What matters is how brand owners choose to respond. This makes speed and agility incredibly important. Act quickly and imaginatively to a situation and you can turn a potentially damaging incident to your advantage. Virgin Trains did this brilliantly on a Pendolino inter-city train. After sitting down and using the toilet a passenger subsequently discovered there was no toilet paper in the cubicle. The passenger tweeted his annoyance and jokingly asked for help. Virgin picked up the tweet, worked out the precise location of the passenger and arranged for fresh supplies to be delivered to his toilet door. The passenger was delighted and the story went viral across a variety of social media channels. By reacting quickly to a single customer Virgin were able to turn a small negative into a large positive media opportunity.

The same logic also applies to fast-moving tech businesses like Uber. They are quickly discovering that what gets you to your first destination or business objective may not necessarily be sufficient for the next. Managing trust is not just about reacting to potentially damaging circumstances. It is also about taking steps to proactively avoid them in the first place. You may offer your customers a great service but that doesn't mean you can get away with having a poor internal culture. In today's business environment the way you behave to your staff is as important as the way you treat your customers. As we mentioned earlier, the better-known the brand, the more customers expect it to observe high levels of good conduct. When your brand has potentially negative social consequences you can't afford to ignore them. You may not agree with the materiality of the situation or even the way the issue is being framed but you must not bury your head in the sand. If Uber appears to ignore the allegations that it is luring Indian taxi drivers into unsustainable commercial relationships, it raises suspicions that it either doesn't care or is blind to the plight of others.

Trust and reputation are especially important in a regulatory environment. The constant flow of negative press sentiment surrounding

Uber's conduct has raised enough suspicion for the Mayor of London and the regulator to use this as the basis to suspend Uber's licence to operate. Whether politically motivated or not, the Mayor has alleged significant safety concerns and expressed serious doubts over Uber's legitimacy. At the time of writing the company has had its licence restored 'on probation', but a failure proactively to address trust issues has provided a basis for challenging what many customers see as a highly innovative and convenient service.

As we have seen repeatedly, if you have a strong brand and a desire to take decisive and restorative action, then in most circumstances (given time) trust can often be either fully or at least partially restored. That doesn't mean that brands can rest on their laurels. Many of the high-profile scandals could have proved fatal if they had affected weaker brands with less robust balance sheets. Trust is hard-fought, easily lost and often costly to restore.

Neither should issues of trust be left to the realms of crisis management. Managing trust is integral to the management of your brand. It is an everyday activity; the constant drip of negative sentiment has the power to fundamentally erode trust even for the most celebrated and innovative companies.

So to conclude; should you ever find yourself part of a serious (but potentially survivable) breach of trust, follow these steps:

1 Act quickly; business, like nature, abhors a vacuum.

2 Take responsibility; offer an unequivocal and unreserved apology.

3 Develop a clear plan to mitigate and resolve the issues at hand.

4 Communicate the plan to all of your key constituencies.

5 Deliver in a style that is recognizably consistent with your brand.

If, however, you have directly insulted your customers, shown a cynical disregard for your own business, instructed your employees to do something completely dishonest or been revealed as a complete fraud, then you may find that trust has completely deserted you.

Of course, the best thing to do is to avoid such an incident in the first place. However, if one occurs the more goodwill you have built for your brand before the incident, the greater the likelihood that your customers will forgive you and give you the chance to rectify the issue.

Further reading

VW the scandal explained: www.bbc.co.uk/news/business-34324772

VW reports biggest annual loss in 80 years: www.ft.com/content/ d777afa0-0893-11e6-b6d3-746f8e9cdd33

Samsung Note 7: www.forbes.com/sites/maribellopez/2017/01/22/ samsung-reveals-cause-of-note-7-issue-turns-crisis-into-opportunity/#1818d30924f1

Virgin www.mirror.co.uk/news/weird-news/man-saved-lack-of-loo-4928118?ICID=FB_mirror_main

What Uber's troubles tell us about the importance of company values: www.ft.com/content/95cebf4a-76d7-11e7-a3e8-60495fe6ca71

Uber's problems in London are Uber's problems everywhere: https://mashable.com/2017/09/22/uber-london-tfl-lost-license/? europe=true

MYTH
3

A STRONG BRAND CAN BE USED
TO PROP UP A BAD BUSINESS

*A brand is not seen as separate or distinct from the
business it serves. They are in fact integral to each other.*

Brands are often credited with powers that they simply don't have.
Chief among these is the idea that a strong brand can successfully
mask the deficiencies of a bad business. There may have been a time
when a strong brand (or strong advertising) was simply seen as a
badge or sticking plaster that could be 'applied' to a business in
order to cover up a myriad of ills, but whatever the historic situation that is certainly not the case today.

The digital revolution of the last decade has effectively left a 'bad'
business with no place to hide. If you are a bad business the chances
are you will be quickly found out. The huge increase in e-commerce
together with the power of social media has combined to provide
a plethora of forums for customers to share their views and experiences. Nothing (it turns out) is as powerful as a third-party
recommendation. A positive rating on Amazon can transform your
commercial success. Specialist websites and publications provide
weekly rankings of the best products or service experiences across

a multitude of categories. Prices can be compared instantaneously and providers compete via programmatic media for your custom.

Against this backdrop it is obvious why a brand can't just be an attractive logo or a nicely packaged product. In today's world we judge a brand by what it does. This has profound consequences, not least for the Chief Executive. If the brand is the sum of everything the business does, then doesn't that make the Chief Executive the ultimate brand guardian?

Image is no longer enough

Even those businesses operating in categories where 'image' has a strong influence on the purchase decision (fashion, tech, luxury etc) will still need to be able to reference distinctive and interesting product attributes. The mobile operator Orange – often heralded as the textbook example of what can be achieved with a strong image – was founded on a democratizing vision that included changing the way customers were billed. Orange was the first mobile operator to bill customers by the second (as opposed to the minute) and this supported their claim to be the UK's first personal network.

So what do we mean by a bad business? Well, 'bad' in this context means a business that is failing its customers. A business that is offering poor quality, a business that is offering poor value, a business that is offering poor choice or is out of step with what its customers want. 'Bad' also extends to the way a brand (or brand owner) behaves, as well as how it treats its staff. None of these things can be masked by good graphic design or great communication.

The importance of staying relevant

Woolworths in the UK serves as an interesting example. A much-loved and – for most of its history – a highly regarded brand,

Woolworths was intimately entwined with the history and growth of Western capitalism. It had a whole series of branded hallmarks, which included the famous Pic'n'Mix – so famous that the phrase finished up entering the common vocabulary – yet none of this stopped Woolworths in the UK going out of business. A 100-year-old retailer went under because it had ceased to be relevant. It wasn't able to offer enough of what its customers wanted. The context had changed; what was previously an endearing and eclectic mix of household products, clothing, music, toys, sweets and entertainment, could now be bought more cheaply and more conveniently elsewhere. A powerful brand couldn't save a bad business.

Take Nokia, the Finnish one-time world-beater, a global leader in mobile technology and the creator of desirable and highly innovative mobile devices. Yet Nokia failed to spot early enough the shift towards the smartphone. Nokia was a hugely respected brand and yet that wasn't enough to stop it losing its ascendancy and yielding leadership to other brands like Apple and Samsung. Microsoft recently sold Nokia for $350m – at the height of its ascendancy it had been valued at close to $300bn. A good brand is not always a good guarantee of future performance.

More recently we've seen businesses like BHS and Austin Reed fail, because they stopped offering enough of what their customers wanted. Before BHS collapsed it had been portrayed as the jewel in Sir Philip Green's empire, hugely successful and highly cash generative and yet in the space of a few short years it ceased to be relevant. New entrants like Primark were proving better attuned to the taste for fast and affordable fashion. Supermarkets were moving into the category and proving highly effective at retailing children's clothing. E-commerce was providing new and innovative ways of shopping online. BHS found itself surrounded and its competitive advantage swiftly eroded. Similarly Austin Reed, another stalwart of the UK high street, just couldn't find its niche. Caught between the new generation of high street fashion retailers and the more upscale luxury brands, Austin Reed's mix of conservative fashion allied to good quality just failed to excite. All that is left of Austin Reed now is an online site and representation at a few outlet stores.

The clothing retailer Gap found to its cost in 2010 that simply using your brand identity as a way of refreshing your business has the potential to cause problems with customers. The mistake Gap made was to try to introduce a new logo without first explaining why the change was necessary. Customers smelt a rat; they believed that Gap was meddling with an iconic identity because it was flat out of ideas about what to do with the rest of its business. The mistake proved costly as in the end Gap was forced to revert to their original logo, an embarrassing and damaging climb down.

The inside matters as much as the outside

A good brand cannot hide a poor internal culture either. Some of the celebrated tech businesses like Amazon and Uber are fast discovering that it pays to treat your staff well. A poor culture can have a number of negative consequences. These can range from poor productivity, through to bad customer service and damaging PR. But it can also cause you big problems at the regulatory and societal level. Even if, as in Uber's case, the majority of your customers love you, it counts for very little if the regulator does not trust you and is suspicious of your culture and values, especially in instances where the regulator has the power to revoke your licence to operate! Customers and regulators are increasingly looking at how a business behaves and how it treats its people, as well as the purpose and values that sit at the heart of an organization.

In today's economy a 'brand' is really shorthand for the way in which the entirety of a business operates. What is the idea that sits at the heart of the business? And how is this evidenced in the way that the business treats its staff, customers and partners?

Rolls-Royce (both the automotive and aero businesses) would not be the well-respected and highly valued brands that they are today without their respective owners investing huge amounts of money in product and service development. Customers believe that Rolls-Royce (in all of its incarnations) stands for quality and engineering excellence, but that wouldn't last long if the cars continually broke down or its turbine engines started malfunctioning or customers continually received bad service. Reputations can be built upon or even enhanced but they can't be faked (at least not for a sustained period of time). Metro Bank – the first new bank to appear on the UK high street in over 100 years – is able to deliver its unique brand of customer service because it treats its staff well and has systems designed to empower (as opposed to constrain) great service. Metro Bank ensures that everything it does is focused on delivering a distinctive service experience.

Using your brand as a sticking plaster to cover up a bad business usually proves counterproductive. What does work is to use a good business to fix a bad (or failing) brand. Fix the brand and it can often amplify and accelerate growth. The automotive sector provides some great examples of this in action. Let's start with one of the most audacious, Skoda.

Fixing failing brands

Skoda Auto was a private Czech business founded in 1895. By 1925 it had become a state-owned company (under communism) and by the 1980s was exporting a range of cheap cars across Europe. It is also fair to say that at that time most Western European markets viewed the Skoda as emblematic of all that was wrong with the communist regime. The cars, while cheap and affordable, were by comparative standards awful. Poor quality, old fashioned, unreliable and slow, perhaps their only redeeming quality was that they were relatively easy to fix. Of course for some families, Skoda did offer affordable motoring. But by the late 1980s even this point of difference was being eroded by the entry-level models of better manufacturers. Skodas were generally treated with derision and in the UK they were regarded as something of a national joke. Then in 2000 Skoda became a wholly owned subsidiary of the Volkswagen Group and things rapidly began to change.

VW wanted a brand that could compete in the value segment but not tarnish the upscale image of VW. They also wanted a brand that was well known across the whole of Central and Eastern Europe. VW realized that they could exploit Skoda's reputation for affordability and then use their own expertise to directly address the product and manufacturing issues. The strategy proved an enormous success. VW started using older platforms and tooling from within their existing portfolio and within just a few months the product was transformed. VW only lightly endorsed Skoda, but savvy customers knew what was going on. Within just a few years (nothing in automotive terms) Skoda went from national joke to a purchase now made by the value-orientated and well-informed. Skoda now represented a fair deal, with reliable engineering and design, utilizing well-established technology at an affordable and highly competitive price.

VW also did something similar with SEAT, the Spanish automobile manufacturer. SEAT started out with a much better reputation than Skoda, but when VW bought the business, it was able to use its heft and resources to improve both the quality and overall attractiveness of the cars. SEAT, already imbued with a degree of Latin flair, provided a means of accessing customers and markets who were turned off by the VW brand, finding it a little too Teutonic or unexciting.

In both instances VW didn't shout about their new ownership. They quietly got on and fixed these businesses. They let the products (the cars) do most of the heavy lifting and it didn't take long for the marketplace to realize that some pretty seismic shifts had taken place. A good business had provided a new context in which these established but underperforming brands could be reappraised. They are now thriving and play a strategically important role within the wider portfolio of VW brands.

The same pattern has been repeated with the Italian motorcycle manufacturer Ducati, often considered as the 'Ferrari' of motorcycles. Ducati was famed for the unique design of its powerful and charismatic engines as well as the beauty of its motorcycles, but they were also notoriously fragile. Small volumes and constrained R&D budgets resulted in unreliable and 'highly-strung' motorcycles. All of this changed when Ducati became part of the VW subsidiary Audi. Money and expertise were used to fix the reliability issues and the business significantly expanded via the introduction of new models aimed at new exploitable niches.

A return to the editor-in-chief

Sometimes it is simply the return of a founder that is enough to rekindle a once successful brand. This is because the brand and the business ought not to be separated. Apple and Starbucks are both businesses that were reinvigorated by the return of their founders. Steve Job's return to Apple heralded a return to form. Jobs quickly realized that for the business to be successful it needed to focus on just a few game-changing products and it needed to champion an intuitive user experience. This, combined with a hate of mediocrity, was sufficient to reset what is now one of the world's most valuable companies. Similarly, the return of Howard Schultz in 2008 saw Starbucks effectively reset its business. Over-extended and less distinctive, Starbucks was damaging its business and its brand. By closing unprofitable stores and refocusing attention back on what was distinctive about Starbucks, both for staff and customers, the business started to recover.

In today's marketplace a brand is not seen as separate or distinct from the business it serves. They are in fact integral to each other. Attempts to use brand identity and advertising as a way of hoodwinking your customers into a poor purchase is likely to prove unsustainable and counterproductive. At the same time if you are a good business and you can apply that virtue to a business and brand that is underperforming you are likely to be able to accelerate the growth and value of your business.

A brand is what a brand does.

Further reading

Skoda has the last laugh: www.telegraph.co.uk/motoring/columnists/neil-lyndon/7922478/Skoda-has-the-last-laugh.html

TECHNOLOGY IS DIMINISHING THE POWER OF BRANDS

Technology is not challenging the power of brands but it is disrupting markets, transforming business and profoundly changing the practice of brand building.

It is often argued that technology is rapidly diminishing the power of brands. The thesis is that technology is undermining the need for us to connect or identify with the brands we prefer and that as technology continues to accelerate there will be little space or need for a brand to exist. We no longer need choice to be simplified by brands; technology can do that for us.

It is easy to see why this argument has captured attention. Brands after all are there to make choice easier. Historically brands have acted as shorthand, a proxy for a much-trusted product or service. Now that it is possible to use technology, or more specifically the internet, to make almost instantaneous comparisons between products and services, what function is a brand really serving? We don't need a brand to simplify choice any more; customers can do that in just a few clicks.

In a situation where customers can seamlessly compare price, features, quality, performance and reliability then surely brands are fundamentally weakened? After all, look at what's happening to the high street. Well-established and often much-loved retail brands are disappearing almost overnight. A decade ago it would have been unthinkable to imagine a global brand like Toys R Us just disappearing, seemingly unable to find a way of making its business profitable and floundering in the face of a new wave of digital arrivistes.

Those that believe in the demise of brands welcome what they see as the re-emergence of the product as king. Now that customers are truly empowered, the thesis goes, all that really matters is the integrity of the product and the willingness (or otherwise) of a customer to advocate for it.

As interesting as all this may sound, it is fundamentally wrong.

Brands as a form of self-expression

As we have already pointed out in previous chapters, brands exist because people like and fundamentally identify with them. Buying something in a modern economy remains a form of self-expression; like it or not, when you buy a product or service you are discriminating, you are exercising choice in favour of one thing over another, you are making your personal preferences known to others and people will (like it or not) be making assumptions about who they think you are. As a consequence our relationship with brands is emotional. Their power vests in their ability to occupy a unique space in our minds. That space might be smaller than it once was but it is still incredibly valuable. A clear set of positive associations residing solely in the mind of the customer is both difficult to displace and difficult to copy.

The continuing need for relevance and distinctiveness

There can be little doubt that technology is making markets more competitive and disrupting many established business models, but there is little evidence that technology is destroying brands. Those evidencing the demise of once-revered names as evidence of the rapidly diminishing power of brands are really just highlighting that a brand (however strong or illustrious its past) is unable to save a struggling business. Businesses like Woolworths, Toys R Us, BHS and Maplin are all examples of businesses that struggled to change fast enough in the face of rapid disruption and a plethora of new competitors. Brands, in contrast, are as important and as relevant as they have always been. The naysayers will argue that, as the role of a brand is to differentiate one company's product or service from that of its competitors, technology is eroding the very basis on which brands are built. The ease with which brands can be compared, combined with the huge demands on our time that technology requires of us, leaves little time for brands to assert their uniqueness. The best a brand can hope for now is to be distinctive. In this age of brand promiscuity, where brands are continually incentivizing us to swap, all a brand can do is try to be easy to find and easy to do business with.

As logical as all this sounds, it doesn't really hold up to greater scrutiny. Across many types of product or service, it is arguable whether customers have ever spent a lot of time in deep contemplation about the relative differences between brands – when buying a can of beans, a chocolate bar or deciding where to buy a coffee, customers have always tended to gravitate towards brands they find distinctive and familiar. Conversely when customers are considering a high-ticket item or planned purchase, such as a car or an expensive piece of audio equipment, then they are naturally more invested in the process (as the consequences are more painful if they make a wrong decision); hence they will often take the time to consider the real points of differentiation between brands.

There is no doubt that technology has made markets more competitive and the role of the marketer more complex, but there is little evidence that the practice of branding is being abandoned or that brands themselves are reducing in number. In fact, as we shall see, the reverse seems to be true.

Meaningful brands generate greater returns

For the past few years the Havas Group have been conducting their 'Meaningful Brands Survey'. This survey looks at the performance of brands that are considered by customers to be more meaningful than other brands operating in the same category. Havas assert that: 'A meaningful brand is defined by its impact on our personal and collective wellbeing, plus its functional benefits.'

The annualized survey has revealed that brands considered to be more meaningful than their competitors generate on average a nine times increase in share of wallet and outperform the stock market average by 206 per cent. Contrary to the naysayers' thesis it seems that customers place a higher value on those brands that have actively sought to build meaning and integrity into the way that they do business, not just given them something more efficiently or cheaply.

Technology is catalysing the creation of new brands

Rather than diminishing brands, technology seems to have heralded a new generation of exciting and disruptive branded entrants. Interestingly, many of the celebrated technology businesses – Google, Amazon, Apple, Samsung, Facebook and Twitter – all seem to have invested heavily in brand building. Indeed, one of the first pieces of advice given to any new tech brand seeking early investment is to make sure they have got their 'story' right. A compelling and pithy expression of their purpose and end benefit is seen as key for those seeking new investment opportunities.

In many instances technology has reduced the traditional barriers to entry and helped new entrants completely reimagine the customer model. This disruption has occurred equally across both business and consumer markets. A huge number of brands have been created and taken hold in the customer psyche.

We have seen the rise of the intermediary brands, that is, those businesses that have grown fast by aggregating the content or output of others. Across categories such as financial services, insurance, air travel, holidays, transportation and entertainment we have seen the arrival of brands like moneysavingexpert.com, comparethemarket.com, expedia.com, opodo.com, trivago.com, trainline.com and stubhub.com. These brands are helping customers to make sense of the huge plethora of choice that exists in the market; they represent a combination of trusted adviser and specialist search aggregator.

Other businesses have completely reimagined whole sectors. Netaporter.com, lyst.com and asos.com are examples of businesses that have transformed premium and mainstream fashion, making the process highly personalized and friction free. Farfetch.com has completely transformed access to couture fashion, acting as a conduit for hundreds of individual boutiques, providing customers with the ability to shop any boutique anywhere in the world.

The same revolution is underway in the business sector. Even professional services, a sector that had until recently proved stubbornly resistant to disruption, is now seeing a plethora of new brands enter the market. The London law firm Lewis Silkin recently launched a new low-cost employment advisory business, Rockhopper, which utilizes technology to offer large businesses high-quality employment advice at highly competitive rates. Market Invoice is a Fintech business that specializes in factoring invoices for businesses struggling with cash flow. Once accepted by Market Invoice a business can use its services (unlike those provided by a traditional bank) in a highly flexible manner. If you type 'crowdfunding' into Google you will immediately be presented not only with a list of the top ten crowdfunding brands but also crowdfunding.com, a business aggregating the best fundraising platforms!

Almost without exception, each of these brands (and these are just a few among many thousands) takes the practice of branding very seriously. Each is taking steps to both broaden and deepen the relationships it has with its customers. None of these businesses see themselves as 'websites'; they are all fully realized brands competing on a daily basis for customers' interest and money.

Technology is providing new opportunities for brand owners

Far from diminishing brands, technology is often helping to promote them. A few years ago McKinsey published its much-vaunted 'loyalty loop' model, describing the sales journey any customer makes from awareness to purchase and then to re-purchase of any product or service. This model asserted that one of the biggest impacts of technology on brands was on the traditional view of the 'purchase funnel'. Prior to the digital transformation of the last ten years, larger businesses tended to structure their marketing activity around a purchase funnel. The initial task was to create significant levels of general awareness, then to persuade the customer to consider your brand, then to get them to prefer you and then ultimately to persuade them to purchase your brand. Different businesses had different versions of the funnel but the main point is that the process was most definitely a funnel; a process that was linear and predicated on the average customer being able to hold (for most categories) five or six brands in their memories. With the impact of digital, McKinsey argued that this funnel had now become in effect a loop.

While a customer may start off (in any given category) being aware of just a few brands, as soon as he or she starts searching the web, the consideration set is almost certain to immediately double. The customer will now be factoring in a new set of brands and will most likely use a combination of rankings and third-party endorsements as a way of reaching their preferred list. At this point the preferred brands should be working hard to incentivize and convert the potential customer. Once the customer has bought the brand, the brand should then provide a mix of emotional and functional attributes to enable the customer to re-purchase and to advocate their purchase to others, thereby closing the loop.

It turns out that technology is in fact increasing the opportunity for more brands to enter the consideration set and in some ways it is asking the brand to tell a deeper and richer story than before. Yes, the product needs to be fit for purpose and the pricing competitive, but discovery, enhanced features and opportunities for advocacy need to be factored into the overall customer experience. All of this adds up to the increasing importance of being able to 'tell' your story. Technology is changing business and asking more of the marketer but it is also providing fertile ground for the creation of new and exciting brands.

If it looks like a brand...

Perhaps it could be argued that many of the largest tech brands aren't really brands at all? Brands like Google and Facebook might 'look' like brands but in reality they are just operating as attractively presented monopolistic entities, working hard to distract your attention away from the fact that you have no real perceived choice. In reality this is inaccurate. Google, Facebook and many other tech brands have acquired their positions through hard work and strong customer appeal. Google became the biggest search engine in the world because it was a much better algorithm than all that had gone before. Facebook went through much iteration before it became the all-encompassing platform that we see today. Both brands do in fact have a host of competitor brands fighting for your attention and more enlightened (or younger) users will deliberately seek alternatives to Google and Facebook. What both these brands have done, however, is use the data they have collected to build impressive revenues and almost insurmountable market dominance.

Brands are used to hold corporations to account

For those that still believe the unstoppable forces of technology are weakening brands, we'd assert that it might actually be the brands themselves that help us strike a new bargain with the technology companies. The thing about highly successful global brands is that they are rarely ignored. In fact we often finish up holding the big brands to a higher level of account than their less well-known competitors. Perhaps that is what we are beginning to witness now. Customers and regulators are beginning to realize the power of these brands and the power that they currently wield. Google and Facebook together receive 75 per cent of all new online advertising revenues. Facebook has allowed third parties access to enormous quantities of customers' data, with profound implications for what we see and interact with while on the platform. These brands will argue that they have done nothing wrong, and they are probably acting under regulatory or legalistic cover, but they need to tread carefully around customer sentiment. As we learn how to navigate this new world, Google and Facebook will undoubtedly be held up to an increased level of public scrutiny, but this is also the power that brands afford; they are a mirror to ourselves.

Technology is not diminishing the power of brands but it is certainly changing the way brands are managed. Branding (as opposed to marketing) has moved from a passive sphere to an active one. The CEO is now best viewed as the most senior brand manager – an editor-in-chief – with the board something more akin to an editorial panel.

Brands are powerful because they help to generate demand and create loyalty. Brands work because they are intimately linked to self-expression. Technology has not changed this. Technology is not challenging the power of brands but it is disrupting markets, transforming business and profoundly changing the practice of brand building.

Further reading

Apocalypse now for Britain's retailers as low wages and the web cause ruin: www.theguardian.com/business/2018/feb/17/uk-retail-industry–gloom-high-street-shift-consumers

Meaningful Brands 2017: https://havasmedia.com/meaningful-brands-reap-greater-financial-rewards/

McKinsey Quarterly 2009: www.mckinsey.com/business-functions/marketing-and-sales/our-insights/the-consumer-decision-journey

**MYTH
5**

BRANDING IS JUST ABOUT
THE LOGO AND ADVERTISING

*A whole chain of experiences that shape perceptions
and preferences creates brands.*

Of all the myths this is perhaps the most enduring, and probably the
most injurious to an appreciation of what a brand is and the different disciplines involved in creating it.

It is easy to understand how it has arisen. The logo and the traditional thirty-second advert on television or the big billboard on the
side of the road are the most obvious and noticeable elements of
any brand's identity. They are also the ones that tend to be most
talked about in the media, which likes to focus on the obvious
parts of a brand as it makes it easier to discuss them with their
viewers or readers. Branding is often associated with the dark arts
of persuasion practised by advertising executives in league with
graphic designers and PR professionals. The hugely entertaining
and popular TV series *Mad Men* is only likely to have reinforced
prejudices amongst its viewers that advertising and logos are what
really create brands.

Of course logos are hugely important, as is advertising. But they are not all that comprises branding. Brand owners don't help greater appreciation of what it takes to build a brand when they make a big splash every time they launch a new logo or change a logo or launch a new advertising campaign and describe what they are doing as creating or changing the brand.

The role of logos and adverts

First, though, we must acknowledge the fundamental importance that the logo plays in the building of any brand. The fundamental purpose of any brand is to differentiate itself so that it is protectable by law. This is for the benefit of its owner and its consumer. The brand name and its accompanying logo or logotype are therefore a fundamental building block of every brand. It is also the asset, the piece of intellectual property that is actually traded when one business sells its brand to another business.

Second, we must also acknowledge that in the past, and particularly in the era in which *Mad Men* is set – the 1950s, '60s and '70s – differentiation in brands came from an artificial projection of a personality or set of imagery and values onto a basically inert product. The traditional equation that was used to explain how brands 'worked' was

$$P + I = B$$

– that is, product plus image equals brand. That would work for any packaged consumer good. So: toothpaste (product) plus confidence (image) equals Colgate. The image was projected onto the product through packaging and advertising; 'confidence' was not an intrinsic product feature, although the product features (fluoride etc) and benefit (fresh breath) were responsible for underpinning or justifying the feeling of confidence.

Given also that the majority of our daily interactions with brands will be with some form of packaged good or advertising on billboards or in magazines or even on your Facebook page, the importance of distinctive and differentiated logos and distinctive and consistent advertising is clear. Moreover, 75 per cent of consumer purchase decisions are made at the point of sale, according to research conducted by The Henley Centre in 2001 and this has remained largely unchanged. The cues that drive us to purchase at the point of sale tend to be the visual ones – the look and feel of the packaging, a strapline or surrounding advertising promoting a particular image or benefit.

But advertising is also important to business-to-business companies. That's why SAP and Accenture run high-profile campaigns in public places like airports. They know that their current and future customers will see them. It reassures people about their strength and capability. The assumption is that if you can afford a big outdoor brand campaign you must be pretty successful or at least have very deep pockets.

So yes, logos and advertising are vitally important in brand building.

But even if branding was simply built through the external or extrinsic expressions of the brand then advertising and logos alone are not enough.

There's more than just a logo in a brand's identity

There are far more elements to managing the brand identity than the logo and a campaign. And many of these elements are in themselves protectable by law as trademarks – assuming, of course, that the brand owners use these other elements consistently and have applied for them to be registered as trademarks. It remains a truth that you can only own legally what you apply to own and what you apply consistently.

Packaging, for example, can be a key legal differentiator as well as a distinctive part of your brand. The (US) Budweiser livery is relatively unchanged over decades of brand management, which the King of Beers (also trademarked) has enjoyed. The graphics, the typefaces, the colours are as recognizable today as they were fifty years ago.

The shape of the Coca-Cola bottle, which was uniquely designed for Coke, is itself the subject of trademark registration. This means that no other cola manufacturer or indeed any soft drink manufacturer can imitate the unique look of the Coca-Cola bottle. In fact the idea of having a very distinctive shape for the Coca-Cola bottle came about precisely because of a fear that the fizzy liquid itself could be easily repackaged and sold under a different name by unscrupulous distributors. Douglas Daft, the legendary and visionary CEO of Coca-Cola during its explosive growth in the early decades of the 20th century, realized that by creating and investing in a bottle which would be difficult for distributors to recreate and which would cost too much money to recreate even if they wanted to, he could protect the interests of both the Coca-Cola company and its consumers.

In Chapter 18 we refer to the battle between the retailers and brands. A key outcome of that battle is that the brand owners, such as Nestlé, invest more heavily in more distinctive packaging shapes, such as the shape of their coffee jars, which they could then protect as a trademark. This not only helps to distinguish the products on the shelves from their own-label competitors, but also suggests an added value or premium product. It crucially gave them a real legal weapon in the battle against what they saw as 'copycatting' by the retailers.

So packaging, and product packaging in particular, is also a key part of a brand's 'make-up'. So are the slogans with which we become familiar. For Coca-Cola 'It's The Real Thing' was for years a famous slogan associated only with them. There are many more that you will have heard of: 'Don't leave home without it'.

'It's finger-lickin' good'. 'The world's favourite airline'. Some of these no longer exist; BA, for example, now uses 'To fly. To serve.' But they remain such important parts of their brands' identities that no one would now consider using them for anything else.

Not only packaging but also the shapes of product design generally can be trademarked and become a part of the ownable elements of the brand. The shape of the Mini has been similar since it first rolled off the production line in the 1960s. Many cars share very similar engineering platforms and often very similar exterior design shapes. Sometimes only the brand's badge on the grill at the front of the car or one or two other smaller features distinguish one car from another. However, the Mini is genuinely unique and its shape is so distinctive that it can't be copied or even near-copied in any way. It is a legally recognized integral part of the Mini brand.

Colours can also be trademarked. The specific colour of Heinz baked beans packaging is a registered trademark. The citation of the trademark registration states that the mark 'consists of the colour turquoise being the most dominant single colour applied to the visible exterior packaging of goods'. Heinz was able to prove that consumers regarded the turquoise colour as so distinctive to Heinz that they would be confused if a competitor selling the same or similar products also used the colour. This 'distinctiveness acquired through use' (the legal expression) enabled Heinz to register its colour as a trademark. The colour purple was so important to Cadbury that it had some success in 1995 in registering it in the UK as a trademark for its chocolate bars. Nestlé have subsequently contested that registration.

Even smells can be registered and protected in use for specific brands because they are part of the distinctive 'make-up' of that brand. The smell of 'Plumeria blossom applied to the thread' was registered as a trademark in the USA by Osewezy, a Californian company that made embroidery thread in 1990, though it has since lapsed. Verizon, the telecommunications firm, has trademarked a 'flowery musk scent' for its consumer stores. In 1996, the UK granted its first olfactory (smell) trademarks to Japan's Sumitomo Rubber Co for 'a floral fragrance or smell reminiscent of roses as applied to tyres' and in the UK, the odour of beer for dart flights by Unicorn Products, a London-based maker of sports equipment. There is some dispute as to how secure such registrations are because of the difficulty of precisely capturing a distinctive smell in words (a trademark must be capable of graphic representation). However, it shows that companies are conscious that consumers use more senses than sight, touch and taste when choosing their brands.

Even music has become an essential part of the brand. Intel's famous signature sound was widely credited as launching the concept of 'sonic branding', the idea that a distinctive sound can be protected by and used to create familiarity, memorability and preference with a specific brand. Jingles have been used for many years by brand owners to create a memorable and emotional connection with their target audience and to help bolster brand awareness. Many of us will still carry in our heads today, like an earworm, jingles we heard from our youth: 'A Mars a day helps you work rest and play', 'Wrigley's Spearmint gum, gum, gum'. The cigar brand Hamlet even successfully applied to have Bach's *Air on a G String* protected exclusively for use in advertising its brand.

Gestures can also be registered as trademarks, though it is rare. Gene Simmons of the band Kiss recently applied to trademark a hand gesture. Compumark, the trademark research and protection business, reported that:

> In 1996, the American professional wrestler Diamond Dallas created the 'diamond cutter' hand gesture – which involved joining the thumbs and index fingers on each hand to create a diamond shape – and later went on to successfully trademark it. When the rapper Jay Z adopted a similar gesture almost a decade ago, Diamond Dallas filed a lawsuit against him on the grounds of trademark infringement, and the case was eventually settled out of court for an undisclosed amount of money.

Protecting these gestures at law is important in maintaining the integrity of the brand and ensuring that they constantly have a recognizable presence. Encouraging consumers to copy these gestures in everyday life is also a way of creating more publicity and recognition for your brand, for free. So all of these and more aspects of the brand identity and imagery and associated and extrinsic attributes are important to building the brand – not just the logo and the advertising.

Brands are built through a chain of experiences

However, all these elements of the management of a brand's identity are but the tip of an iceberg. Of greater importance to consumers or customers is the experience that the brand promises. Failure to deliver and to develop that experience consistently and relevantly can destroy a brand. Kodak did not go out of business because its logo looked dated but because its products were no longer relevant. The same is true of Woolworths and of other retailers who have failed to adapt quickly enough to the changing behaviour of consumers, ensuring that their brand experience matches the promises they once made.

Brands today are built in very different ways than in the times of the Mad Men. Today they are built through the delivery of consistent, recognizable and often remarkable experiences across every touchpoint a customer or a consumer might have of the brand. These include the service style, the method of distribution and the sales and after-sales experience. All of these are integral now to the building of the brand. Largely that is because brands are no longer just consumer products (as we discuss in Chapter 18). If you think about the brands that we experience today, such as Amazon, Starbucks, Google, Facebook, YouTube or even Apple, they are not brands built in any way around a single traditional packaged item bought off a supermarket shelf. And although the logos of each of these brands remain essential and fundamental to them, the role of traditional advertising can vary widely and may not in fact be of any relevance at all.

You might not need advertising at all

Amazon grew its brand not through investment in traditional advertising but by investment in its customer experience. It invested heavily in inventory to ensure that when it started it had more books in stock than the biggest traditional bookseller. A traditional 'bricks and mortar' bookshop might be able to hold around 300,000 books in stock if it has sufficient premises. Jeff Bezos decided that he would hold a million books in stock. He was told at the time that he was crazy to do this because sourcing that number of books would probably cripple his business. He later said that the advice he had been given was both right – it nearly did cripple him – and wrong, because it was also the making of the business. When people realized that they could get any book they wanted on Amazon, the word-of-mouth effect was enormous. And because it was online, people were able instantly to send a link to the Amazon site to a friend rather than give them directions to a store on the street that they might happen to visit the next time they were in town. Bezos has continued to invest heavily in the customer experience, as they have better understood how we buy and what we like to buy. The site is ever more convenient, ever quicker for us to find and receive what we want. The 'One Click' offer was an essential part of that experience. In building the Amazon brand, the experience was becoming the marketing. It is only in recent years, almost twenty years after Amazon was established, that they began conventional advertising. It was simply not relevant enough to how the brand was built before then.

Starbucks is similar. It would be very hard for any of us to recall an advert for a Starbucks coffee shop. There are some adverts for products that Starbucks now sell in supermarket chains, such as its frappé brands. But as Starbucks was growing exponentially globally during the early years of the 21st century, it simply did not advertise. It spent less globally on marketing in traditional terms than Procter and Gamble spent on one product in one market in one year. This is because Howard Schultz understood that consumers' expectations of brands were changing. We are now prepared to pay a premium not for a product benefit or an associated feel-good image, but for an experience that gives us genuine, psychological and practical value. He also understood, like Bezos, that if you get it right, the experience would also be the marketing. The Starbucks stores became not coffee shops but 'third spaces', a place between your home and your place of work where you could hang out, chill out, chat or even work in an environment that was friendly, warm and where you could get coffee. Although coffee was essential, Schultz knew that it was only part of the brand.

Again, think of Apple. If you were to ask anyone what they most associate with Apple, it is unlikely to be the advertising, even though they have produced some iconic adverts in the past, including the classic 1984 Super Bowl ad that transformed perceptions not only of Apple but also of personal computing. It is likely that people will say they associate things such as the iPhone, iMac, the distinctive design, the stores, even the minimalist and functional white packaging design, or perhaps iTunes.

It's likely also that they will mention the Apple store and specifically mention the people who work for Apple. This is important because increasingly the people who represent them, especially the people in frontline service roles, are driving the perceptions of the brand. Many people's perceptions of an airline, for example, will be driven by the way in which they are treated by the on-board air crew and people at check-in. It is why Southwest Airlines, the most consistently profitable and popular airline in aviation history, puts such an emphasis on recruiting the right kind of people, people whom it describes as having 'a warrior's spirit and a servant's heart'. The importance of people in building brand perceptions cannot be overestimated.

Consistently, studies carried out in the UK and USA have revealed that when asked what made any consumer switch from one brand to another, around 66 per cent of the reasons given was the attitude of a person representing the brand or business. It doesn't matter what you say about yourself in your advertising or project through your logo: if the person wearing your uniform or your badge treats the customers or consumers badly, that customer or consumer is likely to leave you for your competitor. They will also tell as many people about their experience as possible on social media. United Airways ran into trouble in recent years when they lost a passenger's guitar. In fact they didn't just lose it, they broke it. What annoyed its owner Dave Carroll most was not that the guitar was lost but his perception of incompetent and uncaring service that he received from the United staff who refused to reimburse him. It prompted him to make a short YouTube video called 'United breaks guitars', which went viral; to this date it has several million views. One commentator, Chris Ayres in *The Times*, even speculated on the cost to United of such bad PR: 'Within four days of the song going online, the gathering thunderclouds of bad PR caused United Airlines' stock price to suffer a mid-flight stall, and it plunged by 10 per cent, costing shareholders $180 million. Which, incidentally, would have bought Carroll more than 51,000 replacement guitars.'

Consistency is vital to maintain your brand

Let's take another brand that exemplifies this changing nature of what makes a brand: a retailer, which also designs and makes products.

Ikea is one of the world's best-known brands. Its blue warehouse stores are identical wherever you go in the world, from China to Canada. Established by Ingvar Kamprad with a purpose of creating 'a better everyday life for as many people as possible', Ikea now has almost 400 stores worldwide and is well on its way to its goal of achieving 500 stores by 2020 and €50 billion in revenue. The success of the Ikea brand lies in its over-performance in a few key moments in the end–to-end customer experience. These are moments which add value to customers and return value to the company. First and foremost are the products themselves: they are the manifestations of the Ikea purpose – affordable Swedish design. They are made in large quantities, which means they can achieve good prices from suppliers. And they are sold in huge quantities at lower prices. It's Billy bookcase is a ubiquitous feature of homes throughout the world; one is reportedly sold every ten seconds. All its products are sold in the same manner in those identical hallmark stores. These do not change noticeably from year to year or from market to market. People visited these stores 915 million times in 2016 and each time they would have had a very similar experience They would have – as we do now – followed the route that Ikea decides: you cannot go off-piste in an Ikea store. The high point is the display of the furniture itself. For many of us, Ikea furniture never looks better than when it is in the store. The stores are often out-of-town sites, so they can take some time to get around and people like to browse in them. So Ikea offers restaurants and family areas. The restaurants serve its famous meatballs, which Ikea also sells in pre-packaged formats in a little food shopping area near the sales counters. Ikea give particular attention to what happens by those counters. It realized that the most stressful part of the journey is often the queuing to pay. So, just beyond the counters, there are small hotdog and ice cream stands, both selling an inexpensive treat which means your last memory, especially if you have children with you, is a nice ice cream rather than the long wait at the checkout.

Ikea's website and catalogue are crucial to its marketing. There were 2.1 billion visits to its website in 2016. And the catalogue is another hallmark of the Ikea brand. More Ikea catalogues were distributed in the world in 2012 than Bibles. Ikea is so conscious of the importance of its catalogue that it has now developed technology that enhances it. You can now get your catalogue online, download it via an app onto your mobile phone and by tapping on the picture of a particular piece of furniture you want and pointing the camera on your phone towards the part of your house where you would like that furniture to fit, it will project the piece of furniture into the room so you can see exactly what is going to look like before you get to the store and buy it.

Ikea is also aware of the importance that its people have in building the brand and makes every effort to ensure that the employees are treated fairly. As Fast Company reported, 'in 2014 Ikea's USA arm used the MIT living wage calculator to determine the hourly rate for its store staff rather than local rates as a result of which 33 of the 40 stores increased wages and 50% of its workforce received a pay bump in 2015'. Happy employees mean happier customers, is Ikea's philosophy. And happy customers become brand advocates as well as repeat custom.

A whole chain of experiences that shape perceptions and preferences therefore creates brands. The logo is always fundamental, advertising is often crucially important but as we have seen in the case of Starbucks, Amazon, Ikea and, as we shall see in Chapter 20, Primark, it is not the essential brand builder. Jeff Bezos famously said a brand is what people say about you when you are not in the room. And what they say about you tends to be the result of what you say and do. In the book *Don't Mess with the Logo,* a brand is defined 'as everything you say and everything you do'. For the modern brand builder in a multichannel world in which people are craving authentic and engaging experiences not just entertaining advertising, remembering to build your brand on everything you say and everything you do is vital.

Further reading

Jon Edge and Andy Milligan, *Don't Mess with the Logo*, FT Prentice Hall, 2009

MYTH
6

BRANDS DON'T HAVE FINANCIAL VALUE

Brands create both economic and financial value.
They are specific assets which generate a security
of income for any business.

In 1988, a little-known but highly successful Australian foods business, Goldman Fettes Wattie (GFW) launched an audacious bid for one of the UK's best-known companies, Rank Hovis McDougall (RHM), owner of much-loved brands such as Hovis bread and McDougall flour.

That bid would start a series of events which would eventually lead to the now long-established practice of brand valuation; the assignment of a specific financial value to any trademark owned by a company. It would mean that, technically and legally, brands – separate from whichever goods or services they endorsed – had financial value.

For the first time, people could prove that brands really did make their owners money. Up to then, brands were not widely regarded as financial assets. Brands and marketing more generally were regarded as costs. And costs whose returns were difficult to prove.

'I know 50 per cent of my money on advertising is wasted,' said Lord Leverhulme (of the original Lever Brothers which eventually merged into Unilever). 'I just don't know which 50 per cent.'

Businesses were valuable, brands weren't. People bought products and products were made in factories. Real tangible things were valuable and so were the real tangible buildings, raw materials, machines and production lines that made them.

Brands were important, of course. You needed to stick a name on your product or else what were consumers going to call it? And you had to advertise it or else how would people find out about it? And it had to be packaged or else how would people see it on a shelf and carry it home? But these were necessary costs of business. They weren't what people were buying. They weren't the value people sought and for which they were prepared to pay a premium.

The limits of league tables

In fact, the myth that brands have no financial or economic value persists today. Despite the fact that the major accountancy boards of the world approve the valuation of brands, despite the fact that the value of brands appears on the balance sheets of major companies, there are still people who think you can't value a brand because a brand is not what people are buying.

A columnist started a recent debate in a UK marketing magazine, claiming brand valuation was 'bullshit' and 'spin'. He based his judgement on the numerous brand valuation league tables that are publicly produced by consultancies as publicity exercises to promote their brand valuation services. These league tables often provide varying valuations for the same brands. And in one notorious case a public valuation of the Nokia brand at $4bn seemed to be undermined when Microsoft, who had bought it for $7bn, actually sold it for just $350m.

The columnist had a point.

But rejecting brand valuation because consultancies might inflate values in a PR exercise would be like rejecting house valuations because estate agencies might occasionally inflate their values in their shop windows. Houses are sold sometimes for more and sometimes for less than the publicly stated valuation. That is how all valuations work. But that does not mean that privately those houses don't have value and can't be valued.

Brands create financial and economic value

Brands create value for their owners. Even the columnist agreed with that. And brands are specific assets – they are intellectual property, properly and securely protected by trademark law. And so like any other asset they can and should be valued. We just don't need to accept the valuation we are given if we are in negotiation to buy them.

But brands aren't just worth a specific financial valuation at a moment in time. Brands have economic value, not just financial value.

There are a few different definitions of economic value. Broadly, one definition is that economic value is the maximum price someone is prepared to pay for something (as opposed to market or financial value, which is the minimum price they might pay). The other definition – much more interesting – is the potential for wealth generation that they bring.

Simply put, financial value means that something can be turned into money. Your house has financial value because someone will pay you something for it. Economic value means something has the ability to generate wealth for you and for others. And that can be harder to quantify but it's still worth trying so to do.

Your house can generate economic value in a number of ways: it requires heating and lighting, decorating and running repairs, so it creates an economy (of plumbers, electricians, painters, plasterers to support it as well as causing you to pay bills to power companies, water companies, the local government etc). It houses people who need to sleep and eat, dress and entertain themselves – so there are beds, fridges, ovens, wardrobes to be bought and filled with food, clothes, books, toys etc. And a house provides a stable home in which people are raised to be good citizens and that means they have a positive impact on the economy.

In other words, financial value is what you are paid when you sell the house; economic value is what you create by what you (or someone else) could do with the house.

And the financial value of the house increases with the economic value of the house. That extension which generated work for the architect, builder, plumber and decorator also puts extra money on the value of the property.

Brands create economic value because of what their owners do with their brands. How they invest in them, how they extend them, how they update them and keep them relevant and fit-for-purpose for their consumers.

Which takes us back to the RHM story.

How brand valuation started

RHM's decision to formally value its brands and place that valuation at the centre of its strategy to defend itself against GFW's hostile bid was forced on it by circumstance and necessity. But the idea of valuing its brands was the audacious brainchild of John Murphy, who was the founder of a small branding consultancy called Interbrand. In his book *Brandfather*, John explains how in 1988 he was on a business trip in Australia when he saw the news story in the country's press about the GFW bid. The idea of an Australian firm buying out a British one had great appeal down under. But John knew intuitively that the appeal of RHM to GFW was not the sense of corporate chest-beating that buying a big British company would allow, nor even the size of the combined companies it would create. The appeal to GFW was RHM's brands. He knew that what

GFW valued about RHM was the value of well-established brands that would give GFW instant and enduring returns on an investment through acquisition.

He had got to the heart of matter: brands were assets that created economic and financial value. They were not just costs of business. The reason for their value was and remains quite simple.

Brands represent a security of future income.

That security is not dependent on any one product. Or any one market. In fact, the product or service can completely change. It can even change from being a product to a service. But as long as the values that customers or consumers appreciate about the brand remain, the brand will continue to have economic and therefore financial value.

Take IBM. Few people would argue that IBM is not one of the world's best-known brand names. But what does it do? It used to make computers. Now it offers consultancy. Virgin is a well-known name, but is it an airline? A fitness centre? A train service? A bank? A range of soft drinks? A bridal service? It's been all of these things and more.

The concept of economic value takes that further. It means they are assets that don't simply have value when they are valued. It means that they create value on an ongoing basis for their owners.

They can do this in a number of ways. For example:

- **Pricing**

  They can enable premium pricing, or at the very least price stability and thus margin stability (if costs are well-managed).

- **Demand generation**

  People want to buy branded goods and services, not generic commodities.

- **Security of demand**

  A customer who is at least satisfied and has no alternative or who is delighted and seeks no alternative will re-purchase the brand at no extra cost of acquisition to the brand owner.

And they add economic value to others:

- They serve repeated needs for customers. In fact, for some customers their brands are vital to their domestic or business life (think where you would be without your Apple computer or your Microsoft Office or if you are a construction business without your JCB digger?).

- They are assets that earn stock market or private investor returns. Imagine what you would have now had you invested even $1 in Apple in 1984 or Amazon in 1995!

- Society welcomes strong brands. When Virgin were awarded their first rail franchise, Richard Branson was told that he had to operate them under the Virgin brand name to give the public confidence in their service.

Brand valuation puts a dollar figure on the amount of money you earn as a business and could be reasonably expected to earn in the future. It ties the soft factors of marketing (awareness, preference, advocacy, image) with the hard factors of finance (earnings before interest and taxes (EBIT), forecast revenues, capital employed). It makes brand performance an enterprise-wide accountability issue, not just a marketer's metric.

Why and how you should put a financial value on your brand

Nic Liddell, the former Head of Brand Valuation at Interbrand, explained this lucidly in the book *Don't Mess with the Logo*. We think it's a good exposition. In the cold, clinical world of valuation, Nic explained, brands are seen as a business asset, like a factory, an assembly line or even a simple biro pen. The argument goes that strong brands create value for their owners because they encourage a higher level of sales (and therefore profit) and because strong brands also encourage a stable, loyal relationship with customers, those sales are more secure in the future. In a nutshell:

strong brands = higher profits at lower risk

Crucially, if the 'brand' is protected by a trademark (or set of trademarks) then it can be bought and sold like any other asset. But unlike most other assets, there is no open market for brands. The price of a factory can be assessed by looking at recent transactions involving similar factories in similar locations (a bit like when you move house), or by working out how much it would cost to buy land and build the factory from scratch. But brands are unique by definition and aren't bought and sold as often as factories, machines and biros. Fortunately many different companies (including the major accountancy firms) have come up with different ways of valuing brands:

- **Looking at the historical cost of developing the brand**

  This is simple, but you need to keep a record of the amount you invest in brand building as that's the brand value. However, it raises the question 'What counts as a brand investment?' Surely more than just marketing spend? Moreover, a lot of brands are decades old, so how do you ensure the records are accurate? And if what you spent is what it's worth then that gives you no return on investment.

- **Considering the value of similar brands**

  This makes sense but brands are supposed to be unique, and 'similar' brands are rarely similar in value. Even in the same category. For example, Coca-Cola's nearest rival Pepsi is only a fraction as valuable.

- **Looking at the cost of replacing the brand**

  This calculates how much you would need to invest to generate similar levels of awareness, sales and loyalty as an existing brand if you had to start from scratch. But given that ultimately you are dealing with behavioural economics (people's behaviour which is affected by many different variables at any given time) it is hard to do this with any logic.

● **The royalty relief method**

By comparing royalty rates charged by 'similar brands' (which can be found in various databases) you could determine what to charge to someone who wants to license the trademark for your brand. However, brands are valuable because they stimulate higher profits and because they reduce risk. The royalty rate method in theory works out what level of profit your brand creates (represented by the royalty), but doesn't tell you anything about risk.

The favoured valuation method, according to international accounting standards, is a discounted earnings (or cash flow) approach:

1 How much of the earnings (or cash) that a business is forecast to generate can be attributed to the brand?

2 What level of risk should be associated with these forecast brand earnings (or cash)?

1 How much of the earnings (or cash) that a business is forecast to generate can be attributed to the brand?

Brand preference is always important but it is more important in some categories than in others. In fact, people might not like your brand very much but still be forced to buy you for other reasons. For example, take petrol stations. You might not like Shell very much, you might prefer BP (or vice versa) but if your car needs petrol you are going to fill up at the nearest station regardless of who owns it. Whereas if you like Chanel No 5, you'll buy Chanel No 5; you won't just get something to make you smell nice. So 'brand preference' is less important in the petroleum industry than in comparison it is in the perfume industry.

Therefore, to work out how much of your earnings are due to people preferring your brand, you have to separate the earnings the business makes into 'tangible' and 'intangible' ones (tangible means things like factories, equipment, the petrol stations and the petrol you might own etc – ie things you can touch). And then identify how much of the 'intangible earnings' are generated by your brand as opposed to other intangibles such as patents, distribution agreements etc.

2 What level of risk should be associated with these forecast brand earnings (or cash)?

People might prefer your brand but do they 'demand' you? Take banks as an example. A lot of people use Barclays but there is little evidence that most people love them. Whereas, in the UK, First Direct or Metro Bank have loyal customers who recommend them. So security of demand for the Barclays brand might be comparatively lower than that for First Direct or Metro Bank.

Therefore, you have to identify how strong the loyalty and affinity to your brand are with your customers and also the other factors that affect that demand, such as how available you are. Accountants can use an analysis of that strength and turn that into a risk rate. By applying that risk rate to the forecasted brand earnings for a number of years into the future and adding those earnings up, you get a Net Present Value. And that is the financial value of the brand – assuming someone is prepared to pay that for it. Figure 1 shows the process.

Mythmakers might ask why brands in utilities or petrochemicals but which are not everyday consumer goods are, in brand

Figure 1   Brand valuation: The Interbrand approach

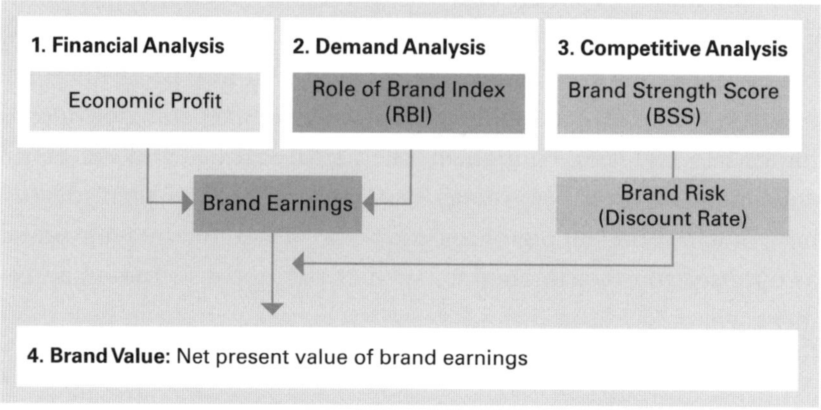

NOTE Interbrand was the first company to have its methodology certified as compliant with the requirements of ISO 10668 (requirements for brand valuation) as well as playing a key role in the development of the standard itself.

valuations, worth more than brands that everyone knows, like Chanel. The answer is that petrol is bigger than perfumes. For example, BP's turnover in 2017 was $240bn, the tenth time in recent years that it had exceeded $200bn a year. In 2017, Chanel's turnover reached $10bn for the first time. Demand for Chanel by its consumers might be higher than demand by BP's consumers for its brand, but that means the Chanel brand will be worth a higher percentage of a lower total value than BP. BP is still going to have the higher brand value financially.

This difference was manifested through Interbrand's own league tables in 1996. In their book *The World's Greatest Brands*, Interbrand ranked McDonald's first because that book looked at brand strength only. But in its brand value league table published the same year in *Financial World*, it ranked McDonald's third with a value of $18bn behind Coca-Cola (second place in both tables) and Marlboro which was 1st according to brand value ($44.6bn) but which was tenth according to brand strength. Why was this? Well, because even today the global cigarette market remains bigger than the global cola or fast-food restaurant market. In 2016, according to various sources, the global cigarette market was worth $683bn, the soft drink market $286bn and fast food $539bn. We still buy more smokes than sodas, more fags than fries.

So a healthy brand value shows that you've got a great brand that's being supported by a great business in a great market. A low brand value means that the brand is weak or the business is weak or the market is weak. It's impossible to tell which unless you look at the detail of the valuation.

Mythmakers also say that 'brand valuation is subjective'. And it is. Valuations are always educated guesses no matter what you are valuing – a house, a car, a factory. This is no different when analysts value entire companies. They try to forecast earnings or cash flow and they also try to estimate how risky those earnings are. Just like analyst valuations, brand valuations represent an expert's opinion of how valuable a brand is.

For most companies, the exact brand value itself is of secondary importance. What's more important is that a good brand valuation methodology considers lots of types of data from different sources – including financial and marketing data – and brings these together into a single framework. Even if the valuation achieved isn't perfect, the process you need to go through to get to it forces you to think hard about how and where your brand creates value. It gets the finance team and the marketing team talking the same language. And it can be updated each year so you've got a way of understanding how well you've done in achieving your goals and what goals you should be setting in the future. If the value is big and impressive enough, you can put it in your Annual Report to make your shareholders happy, or you might even benefit from the free publicity that comes with inclusion in one of the many brand value league tables that are published in prestigious titles like *Business Week*.

Companies have used brand valuation to transform their businesses:

- moving the brand to the centre of their businesses to ensure alignment with all operations
- to help divest those businesses that may be fundamentally sound, but are no longer core to building the brand
- to improve their financial reporting and show the true value of the businesses
- to help explain to everyone who works for and with them what a great brand they have and what value it generates for the business

Einstein is supposed to have said: 'Not everything that counts can be counted, and not everything that can be counted counts.'

True.

But that should not stop us from counting what we should count – even if our counting might be, well, a very good best guess.

Further reading

John Murphy, *Brandfather: The man who invented branding*, Book Guild Publishing, 2017

Jon Edge and Andy Milligan, *Don't Mess with the Logo*, FT Prentice Hall, 2009

DIFFERENTIATION IS DEAD. DISTINCTIVENESS MATTERS

The truth is you need to both differentiate and be distinctive. You actually can't do one without doing the other.

This is a modern myth, which needs either squashing or at least clarifying. It stems from what we believe is a partial reading of an excellent book called *How Brands Grow: What marketers don't know* by Byron Sharp. *How Brands Grow* captures in one place much of what we think about brands and makes some very pertinent and sensible recommendations.

However, we think there have been some modern mythmakers who have latched on to a couple of its conclusions for probably their own purposes. The book argues that brands grow because they are associated with a few things that really distinguish them in the minds of consumers, not one differentiator. And effectively it also argues that brands that spend a lot of money on marketing also grow best.

The latter conclusion is very persuasive to people in advertising agencies and of course in marketing departments who are facing greater scrutiny on effectiveness of spending and even shrinking budgets. It must seem like a lifeline at a time when big brand owners are questioning whether traditional advertising agencies can give them the help they need in the modern world.

It's the wording of the myth – distinctiveness matters, differentiation doesn't – that worries us.

What's the difference between differentiation and distinctiveness?

First of all, let's try to get some definitions agreed. Because part of the problem is that people are using different meanings for the words 'differentiation' and 'distinctiveness'. In fact, the way people are giving meaning to these words reminds us of the discussion between Humpty Dumpty and Alice:

> 'When I use a word,' Humpty Dumpty said, in rather a scornful tone, 'it means just what I choose it to mean—neither more nor less.'
>
> 'The question is,' said Alice, 'whether you can make words mean so many different things.'
>
> 'The question is,' said Humpty Dumpty, 'which is to be master – that's all.'

At the moment, it seems that the 'master' meaning for some people in marketing is Byron Sharp's:

> Differentiation (a benefit or 'reason to buy' for the consumer) and distinctiveness (a brand looking like itself) are different things.

He then goes on to say:

> This isn't just semantics, as any lawyer or judge will tell you. Distinctiveness (branding) is legally defensible, while differentiation is not (other than time-limited patent protection).

Well, we think these are in fact fine splitting of semantic hairs. If you go to any dictionary or thesaurus, you will find that differentiation and distinctiveness are closely associated (in fact a dictionary definition of differentiation is 'the action or process of differentiating or distinguishing between two or more things or people' and a dictionary definition of 'different' is 'distinct').

Branding has always sought to differentiate, and it has done so by being distinctive.

The truth is you need to both differentiate and be distinctive. You actually can't do one without doing the other.

The three rules of differentiation

Roberto Goizueta, who was one of Coca-Cola's most successful CEOs, famously gave his three rules for successful brand building:

Differentiate, differentiate, differentiate.

Brands exist by law to differentiate one supplier from another. That is why we have trademark law. It ensures that appropriate differentiation is legally defensible, allowing any supplier to protect their trade against imitation or counterfeiting by another. It also ensures that any purchaser (customer or consumer) is buying or using a bona fide good or service.

If we were to give an order and more meaning to Goizueta's three rules, the first would be to differentiate through your brand name. You have to create a brand name that nobody else in your market can copy. It has to be that different. It has to be different from any generic terms that apply to your market or should be allowed to be used by anyone to describe distinctive aspects of their goods or services. So, if the distinctive aspect of your delivery service is speed, you nevertheless could not register and protect as a trademark the word 'fast' or 'speedy'. You would have to add another word to it or create a neologism like 'Fastrak' or 'Speedline'. Anything to differentiate it from the generic term which other companies who could show that their delivery service is also fast should be allowed to use.

That's why so many companies develop or choose such distinctive names. They need to be genuinely different from anything else: Ocado, Amazon, Xerox, Fatbrain, Moonpig. Then you can more easily protect your business and your consumer by law.

The second rule of brand differentiation would then apply to all the other aspects of the brand's identity or expression: the logo, the colours, the imagery, the packaging shape, the copylines etc. In the end, people need help through brand differentiation to find what they are looking for quickly on the shelf or on the street (think of those Golden Arches). Branding can even help people choose because they prefer one colour or one image to another. Some people like red and some like blue. Or it can help to signal and segment a product for different users. Coke is red, Diet Coke is silver. For many years, Unilever produced the Head & Shoulders shampoo brand targeted at men who were concerned about dandruff. Eventually, they decided to launch a version targeted at women. There wasn't a huge difference in the formula. They changed the fragrance and crucially differentiated it by packaging colour – they made it pink for women, differentiating it from the original blue which remained broadly for men. This kind of differentiation helps consumers quickly to find you, recognize you and remember you.

We can all think of brands that we recognize and thus are able to differentiate purely on their logo alone. In fact, so distinctive because so different are their logos, that we don't even need to see the whole logo – one letter or one half of the logo will give us the clue we need. Just a sight of the top of those Golden Arches viewed 500 yards in the distance will have a child pestering parents for McDonald's. We're sure you can think of many (that chunk out of the side of the Apple logo, any of the three letters of IBM, the D of Disney). In fact, there are board games and online games based entirely around guessing the logo. That is differentiation. It's also distinctiveness.

The third rule of differentiation would be what we would call the 'meaningful' differentiation, the reason you buy or prefer a brand because of something that they do which particularly appeals to you. And this is where the overlap with genuine distinctiveness occurs.

Most people choose to fly Ryanair because of price. But it is not the only low-cost carrier and sometimes it might not even be the cheapest on any given route. But low price is a distinctive part of the Ryanair brand. It might not differentiate them technically or legally in the way that the Ryanair brand name and associated trademarks do, but it distinguishes them so significantly that it contributes to an overall sense of difference in the market that gives people a reason to buy them.

One of the other reasons why pricing distinguishes Ryanair is because generally they do it better than others. And being 'better' or at least being perceived to be 'better' is a differentiator. In the automotive industry, German cars have a perception of being better 'engineered'. BMW, Mercedes-Benz and Volkswagen have collectively benefited from the decades of focus on quality performance through engineering and also from the general perception that Germans are good at high-quality engineering and production. Some of these perceptions can be tested and proved. It was Karl Benz who, in 1879, first patented the internal combustion engine and then in 1886 received a patent for his first automobile. *Fortune* magazine wrote that the German automakers' brand strength was founded on their focus and commitment to engineering excellence. For example, BMW had a goal of building every vehicle with a 50–50 weight distribution. And *Fortune* also noted that 'Engineers occupy a high pedestal in a country that prizes technology and craftsmanship.' So the culture of the country supports the perception of the customer.

The main reason we chose Ryanair as an example, though, is because it is not a consumer product brand. And many people often associate brands with consumer products. When in fact brands are, as we explain in Chapter 18, not just packaged goods.

Being meaningful

Byron Sharp refers to meaningless distinctiveness rather than 'meaningful', by which he means that people like a brand simply because they like it. They might summon up some post-rationalization of their preference but essentially it's an emotional choice. Sometimes the choice may have been made in childhood so long ago that they cannot remember why, let alone when they first chose the brand. Many of us, for example, have a favourite breakfast cereal or chocolate bar which we have had since we were kids. Just like our favourite sports teams or celebrities.

Football clubs are also brands, and for many of us our choice of our favourite football team is largely accidental or emotional either by birth or because the team had a player we liked or a strip we liked. There is a Plymouth Argyle supporter who was born in Birmingham and has no relations with Plymouth at all. But when he was five years old, he saw the Plymouth Argyle club badge (the Mayflower ship that carried the Pilgrim Fathers to America) and liked it so much that he liked the team. He has supported them ever since because he liked their logo. Now that is brand loyalty. And it is probably a good example of meaningless distinctiveness.

We don't really like the phrase 'meaningless' distinctiveness because it suggests that an irrational or emotional motivation is not 'meaningful' or valuable. We'd argue that emotional motivation is extremely rational; it might not be logical, but it is extremely rational. Fear, love, hate, kindness all stem from perfectly rational responses to situations or people. Nostalgia, a sense of personal identity and a sense of belonging to or a shared way of looking at the world with others are all also perfectly rational for human beings.

But we very much agree with Sharp – even if we don't like the term 'meaningless' – we buy emotionally and then justify our purchase rationally. And to buy emotionally, we need to see, appreciate and recognize something that is distinctive.

Being remarkable

Oscar Wilde once said, 'There is only one thing in the world worse than being talked about, and that is not being talked about.' That is very true for brands. It is now more important than ever to be distinctive and to be recognized and recommended for being distinctive, for being remarkable. To be, in one of our favourite phrases, 'top of mind and tip of tongue'. According to research by the Ehrenberg-Bass Institute (from which the book *How Brands Grow* emerged), customers are spending less time thinking about the subtle differences between brands, and instead are interacting with the brands they find interesting and distinctive. But there is no surprise there. Did any of us ever spend lots of time contemplating the relative uniqueness of Coca-Cola over Pepsi Cola?

There were, famously, blind taste tests conducted during the 1970s and 1980s, which PepsiCo repeatedly used to demonstrate that more consumers actually preferred the taste of Pepsi to Coke. Consumers were given glasses of unbranded cola and asked to rate which they preferred. Apparently, Pepsi outscored Coke because Pepsi's formula produces a taste which is a little softer and sweeter on the palate. But slap the respective branding on the cans, stick it on the supermarket and local store shelves and millions more will still buy Coke. Not least because Coke, being the bigger brand, has more marketing muscle and money. Pepsi even recruited David Beckham to be its brand ambassador, but that did not change the situation.

The fact is people know what is distinctive, familiar and recognizable about Coke, they know what they are going to get even if they can't logically explain it clearly and comprehensively. The distinctiveness of the Coke brand, enshrined in the protectable differentiation of its trademarked brand identity, outperforms the differentiation offered by Pepsi's apparently 'better' taste.

Our approach to choosing our brands based on an overall sense of their distinctiveness rather than a series of specifically differentiated features and benefits applies to every sector. From your local supermarket to your online retailer. From your airline to your automobile. Are you more prepared to consider the contrasting claims of alternative brands than you used to be? Do you like having brands compete for your attention? Or do these questions never trouble your thoughts? The truth is we never had much time to interrogate these differences and increasingly we have less time and more choice and, in this context, being memorable, being distinctive is the only thing that matters.

As consumers we have never spent our time thinking deeply about the various claims to differentiation with which companies bombard us. Rather, when contemplating a brand, we have always connected with a feeling or an association, something distinctive underpinned by a specific set of features or benefits. Something that made us feel good and would give us things to talk about.

What has changed is the relentless focus, energy and imagination now demanded of brand owners to remain distinctive and therefore remarkable and re-purchasable.

What brands 'own' and what they 'occupy'

In the debate about this confusing myth we prefer to distinguish between what brands 'own' and what they 'occupy'. What brands own is what differentiates them legally. Brand name, logo, logotype, colours etc. And possibly some associated patented technologies such as the swipe feature on an Apple phone's screen (though these have a limited life).

Brands build distinctiveness by what 'space' they occupy in our minds. Volvo is no safer than other major motor manufacturers but if you were to ask a group of middle-aged car drivers what the attribute is they most associate with Volvo, it's likely to be safety. That is because for years they focused on communicating that to car drivers.

As with owning a house, you own the freehold (or leasehold). But a distinctive home is what you occupy – the way the house in which you live is designed, built, decorated and filled with fixtures and fittings. All of those create the distinctive character of the house and can be changed or even lost. The legal title to living on that plot of land endures even when the house collapses.

Successful brands focus consistently on an image and an experience that they want to be recognized and valued for by customers or consumers and indeed by other groups of people, especially employees. Apple does not 'own' creativity, cool design and human- or user-friendly products. Samsung can lay claim to these things too. But Apple has created a distinctive brand around these attributes by the focus they have put on them. The clean monochromatic styling of their products and stores, the signature graphic and product designs, the tone of voice ('Hello', 'Designed in California'), the informal, friendly style of their people, the emphasis on entertainment, the 'wow' effects they bring at launch. All of these form a distinctive impression of the Apple brand which most of us would struggle to articulate clearly but which we all know and recognize and with which many identify.

In the same way, Nike does not 'own' in any legal or otherwise proprietorial sense the ideas of 'exceeding your personal best', of irreverence, of performance, of energy. Adidas and Nike both have high-performing athletes on their books, they both make products with sports science and technology-inspired features, and they both make impressive adverts which feature ordinary people and stars. And other brands like O'Neill, Converse, Puma and Reebok are all capable of doing and talking about similar things. But Nike has occupied that space in our minds by relentless focus, by a clear artistic and design ethos that brings an edge to all their branding, by their audacious marketing and of course by their readiness to spend money to support it. As a result, they have emblazoned on our minds three things they really do own: the Nike name, the swoosh logo and the slogan 'Just Do It'.

How to be remarkable

So, to be remarkable, where do you focus and how do you do it? The answer lies in three simple principles. These principles are ones identified in the book *On Purpose: Delivering a branded customer experience people love*. The book recommends that if you want your brand to remain relevantly distinctive and be part of consumers' consideration and conversation, then it needs to stand up, stand out and stand firm.

Stand up – means having a purpose or cause, which brand owners pursue consistently and talk about constantly. A purpose that they believe will deliver true value to and improve the lives of their customers or consumers and the world in which they live.

Stand out – means that they dramatically differentiate and distinguish their brands from competitors by intentionally delivering a repeatable and remarkable experience across all channels or touchpoints for their customers or consumers.

Stand firm – means they create, maintain and develop the appropriate culture to ensure sustainable and authentic delivery over the long term.

In Chapter 5 we give a couple of examples of brands that have built highly distinctive associations in our mind through their relentless focus on these key principles, well-known brands like Ikea. Here, to illustrate the point about distinctiveness, we'll take one example from a sector about which consumers rarely have anything good to say – banking. In 2010, Metro Bank became the first new UK high street bank to launch in almost 150 years. It has fast become one of the sector's most positively talked about businesses and one of its most successful.

Stand up

Metro Bank understands that first you have to know what it is you want to be remarkable for. You have to champion what matters most to your customers and build your offer around that. During the last decade of the previous century and the first decade of this, banks were increasingly withdrawing from the high street, closing branches, investing less in the experience of many of those branches and encouraging more online and telephone banking. They were also increasingly developing new financial products and more complex financial services, straddling retail, corporate and investment banking. It became difficult to know what the focus of these banks was. It certainly did not seem to be the customer, judging by the dissatisfaction of many customers with their banks.

Metro Bank came to this market with a purpose and a simple clarity. They were going to be branch-led because they believed bank branches had a role to play in a community and thus in a customer's life. A report by Mintel appears to support their belief. It recorded that 84 per cent of customers liked to go to their bank branch either frequently or regularly, with 25 per cent saying they would not even consider a bank that did not have a branch. Metro also decided to focus on the products that matter most to customers. They focus on current accounts, savings accounts and credit cards for customers or companies. They have a clear sense of who their core customer is: an average person who wants to go to a bank that is easy to do business with. They were going to champion customers and they were going to make people 'love going to their bank'. Metro Bank uses language customers can remember; it is 'a bank that puts you first'. In fact, it doesn't talk about customers; it talks about fans, a simple premise that is revolutionising UK high street banking.

Stand out

To get people talking about you, you have to do something worth talking about. Metro Bank doesn't offer the most competitive rates of return, but it purposefully invests in what its customers most value. It has done so by looking at what was wrong with traditional bank branches and creating something directly opposite to that. Old bank branches opened at a time that suited banking (9am–5pm Monday to Friday, Saturday mornings if you were lucky). Metro has convenient opening hours for its customers (8am–8pm Monday-Friday, 8am–6pm on Saturdays and they are even open 11am–5pm on Sundays). Old banks had stern-looking staff behind glass windows (presumably to protect the staff as much as the money). Metro has friendly staff who walk around the store and sit at open desks. Applying to open a bank account at an old bank involved an agonisingly long process of paperwork, references, and waits while checks and double-checks were conducted. Metro Bank offers instant account opening – you can walk into a branch and come out within an hour with a new bank account ready to use. Old banks were about as family-friendly as a morgue. Metro Bank lets dogs in (even providing water bowls) and kids can play on a Magic Money Machine. Its branches are easy to find and easy to do business with.

Stand firm

Metro Bank knows that it is not for everyone and it is comfortable with this. It knows that delivering a remarkable customer experience requires a business to make choices. Its systems are designed to empower staff. It has a simple service ethos: it takes one person to say yes to a customer and two to say no. Staying true to its promise is yielding significant results. It puts an emphasis on service style and attitude in its recruitment and encourages informality and fun within its culture.

Adhering to these principles and supporting them with PR and social media means its customers have done much of the talking for them. Metro Bank has spent less than £100,000 in conventional advertising in six years but has brand recognition of 82 per cent. It helps that it sees its big, bold, modern-looking, highly branded stores as living advertising billboards on a high street.

Metro Bank has grown in less than a decade to be an influential force in the banking industry and an increasing presence on the high street; with deposits of £11.7bn and a loan book of £9.6bn, 55 branches and 1.2million customers. When you consider that the Mintel study cited earlier indicated that the main banks have lost over three million customers, it seems that Metro's focus on being distinctive and different is paying off.

So, it's not that a brand needs to be distinctive rather than different. It needs to be both. But it needs to focus on what will make it genuinely distinctive and keep focused on delivering that consistently. The combination of that plus the constancy of protecting the brand identity that it owns, and which genuinely differentiates it, makes it remarkable.

Robert Stephens, the founder of Geek Squad, which quickly became the leading provider of domestic IT services in the USA, says: 'Marketing is the tax you pay for being unremarkable.'

Brand owners should ask themselves how much 'tax' *they* are paying.

Further reading

Byron Sharp, *How Brands Grow: What Marketers Don't Know*, Oxford University Press, 2010

Shaun Smith and Andy Milligan (2015), *On Purpose: delivering a branded customer experience people love*, Kogan Page, 2015

MYTH
8

THE CUSTOMER
IS ALWAYS RIGHT

The right way to think for brands is:
'The right customer is always right.'

Some myths are based in truth and reality. There really were cities that sank into the sea, like the myth of Atlantis (it's just we're not sure if Atlantis was one of them). The 'customer is always right' myth is almost true but the 'almost' makes it a dangerous myth to be taken literally.

The right way to think for brands is that 'the *right* customer is always right'.

Many companies talk laudably but quite meaninglessly about putting the customer first. In more companies than we care to think about, there are value statements, which include being customer-focused. The truth, in our experience, is that for too many companies, customers are not their top priority. Shareholders are. Even though those shareholders will only make a decent return if they have growing and profitable revenues, which only come from having customers. And also from having engaged employees. In 2011, the Temkin Group conducted a survey of employees working for all kinds of companies, and concluded that as many as 99 per cent of employees who worked for businesses who were genuinely customer-focused agreed that they were 'committed to helping their company succeed'.

Not all customers are right for you

Part of the problem is that companies do not spend time thinking about who their target customer is and building a value proposition around them. They often regard all customers alike and are happy to have as many of them as they can get.

But a successful brand will not treat all customers equally. The first thing successful businesses do is understand who their most valuable customers are. This is not the same as knowing who your largest group of customers is. Because it might be that you have lots of customers who are simply not profitable enough for you. The Pareto Principle that 20 per cent of anything will deliver 80 per cent of something is in its broadest sense true for business customers. That's why it is important to segment your customer audience, understand which of them are the most valuable. Typically, they are the ones regularly purchasing from you, often purchasing new offers from you, giving you extremely high scores of satisfaction and advocating for you. Such customers are often called 'fans'. O2, the telecoms operator in the UK, had a 'fandom' index to help it understand not only who were its top customers but also how much O2 was doing to keep them satisfied. However, do not make the mistake of over-segmenting into such micro-groups that it becomes impossible to do anything meaningful with them.

If you treat all customers the same, you end up losing focus and becoming neither differentiated nor distinct. If you don't mean something to somebody, you mean nothing to anyone.

In the past, some prestigious brands have allowed their value to be diluted because they were not selective enough about their target customers.

Burberry found its brand was both being associated with groups of customers who did not reflect their desired image and beginning to put off the customers who would. As the *Daily Mail* reported in 2008:

Burberry became too ubiquitous for comfort, and soon the distinctive house check was adopted as a badge of honour for the newly emerging chav generation.

The day that former soap star Daniella Westbrook and her daughter stepped out head to toe in Burberry sounded the death knell for the company's credibility. It had to change, and it had to change fast.

Sadly, it seems we are fashion snobs who like people like us to wear the clothes we like. Burberry turned that round by rediscovering its brand purpose, reinvigorating its creative offer, transforming its customer experience and encouraging the right kind of customers. Its classic The Art of the Trench campaign was a great example of that.

Other companies have taken dramatic and symbolic action to show what kind of customers they value and what kind they don't. Herb Kelleher, the CEO of Southwest Airlines for the majority of its time as the leading low-cost carrier, tells the following story. A customer wrote to Southwest complaining in strong language about the behaviour of one of its staff. Southwest take their responsibility to their employees very seriously: 'culture is king' at Southwest. So they did not take the complaint lightly and investigated thoroughly. Not only did they conclude that there was no case to answer and that the employee had behaved appropriately, they went further. They wrote to the customer, informing them of the outcome of the investigation, dismissing the complaint and told the customer that they would no longer be welcome on any Southwest flight.

That customer was very much not right.

Six Senses is a luxury resort chain which has a strong environmental offer. When you visit one of the resorts you are asked to step back a little from civilization. No shoes, peace and quiet. It's not a place for someone who wants every kind of modern convenience or 'bling-style' luxury. One customer hated it so much she started complaining about everything to all the staff and to the manager and also other guests. Rather than agree with her complaints or adjust any of their service, the General Manager arranged a helicopter to take her off the island to a resort that was more to their liking.

Again, that customer was not right.

There are of course also customers who make bogus complaints and false claims in the hope of getting compensation. Though these are relatively rare. In fact, employee theft is a bigger threat than customer fraud to most companies. Most companies have good ways of spotting those customers who are not right.

Many companies conduct periodic reviews of their customer base. When done well this can be helpful for customer and company alike. For example, you may have received notification from your gas or electricity or TV/broadband supplier, suggesting you go on a different tariff more suited to your needs. Banks are particularly keen on this, although it can lead to some unexpected shocks. A review by one bank of its business customers led to them closing several accounts because they no longer fitted with the business strategy (ie were not big enough accounts to be worth retaining) and as a result they gave six weeks' notice of closing to a company who had been their customer for almost twenty years. There are better ways of saying goodbye.

Get to know the customers who are right

As the expression goes, 'Shoot where the ducks are flying!' Make sure you're focusing effort on the areas of highest proper potential, not throwing away your valuable time with those customers who do not have the potential to affect your company's performance positively and who take up too much of your time. Inevitably, over-servicing less valuable customers will mean underservicing the valuable ones, the ones that do positively affect your business. That is not a good place to be.

One of the challenges in finding and serving appropriately the right customers is to live with the ambiguity that not all customers are equal but every customer might have equal potential. So you need to establish what the future value of your customers is to create an initial priority list. You need to grade your customers – let's say ABCD. This is a good recommendation given by David Kean and Chris Cowpe in their book *How To Win Friends and Influence Profits*. Grading customers will help you to determine where to focus your resources and effort. It will also help you not to waste time holding on to customers that sap your energy and, even worse, dilute rather than enhance your margin.

The A List customers are the key strategic targets on which the brand's energy must be deployed most effectively in pursuit of organic growth. Your brand will have a very strong relationship with these customers and they will be strong advocates for you and in the wider customer community, through social media. You will be already giving these customers your best products or services but you can also use them to test and trial new opportunities. Better still you can spend time getting to know them closely – through qualitative, quantitative or ethnographic research, preferably in real time – so you can identify other needs or wants they might have of you. They can also highlight areas of your brand which need improving and can even give you feedback on what they think of as your competition, which might surprise you. These customers are very much right!

B customers will be ones with whom your brand enjoys good solid relationships and where there is a good level of activity but not as dynamic and fast-growing as with A clients. They may be slower moving. They may take time to adopt new offers or change habits. But they can also be the bedrock of your customer revenue and as such it is essential that you invest in them.

C clients have a serve and maintain status. You may well have a good relationship but they will never have the brand boosting and revenue potential of A and B clients. They are nice-to-have customers to whom you will continue to provide a solid (but not a special) service and in which you would not overinvest ahead of revenue. You may decide to cull such customers (as the bank mentioned above did) but the risk to your brand reputation might not be worth it.

D customers should probably be culled from your list. They will be margin diluters. They will sap the energy of your frontline colleagues because they will never be satisfied with your service. They will quibble over bills or the prices and will constantly moan about you on social media. It takes courage and costs some money (as in the case of Six Senses and its helicopter) to lose them. But it will be worth it. It is rumoured that one of the most successful consulting firms in the world culls the bottom 10 per cent of its customer base every year. It does not seem to have hurt them.

Of course, to understand who your most valuable customers are you also have to understand whether you are creating or giving them things that they value. So it is important to research with your customers what you think of them and also what they think of you. There is no point trying to focus on your A customers if those clients actually don't value what you are giving them.

Nevertheless, one of the most important things that any business can and should do is to ensure that they are removing customers or clients who are of no value to them. Unprofitable customers create unprofitable businesses and unprofitable businesses do not last.

Consumer brands can learn a lesson from business-to-business brands

Most of the examples we have given in this book are from well-known consumer brands. So we think it's important to share an example from the business-to-business world because brands are just as important in that sector.

In *How to Win Friends and Influence Profits*, Kean and Cowpe share the story of a law firm in London which grew dramatically by identifying which customers were the 'right ones'.

The Head of Business Development at this law firm worked with her senior partners to assess how many of over 1,000 clients were actually profitable. It turned out only 3 per cent of the client base were regarded as profitable, so were called Level One Prospects. They were selected not only on the basis of current and future revenue potential but also on the strategic importance to the firm. A similar exercise revealed a further 70 clients were Level Two prospects in sectors where they wished to make inroads or deepen their penetration. The firm decided that the hierarchy of Level One and Level Two prospects should not mean that the service received by these respectively was superior to that received by others. The point of the exercise was not to rebalance the efforts of expertise of the firm in a professional capacity, it was simply to reprioritize where and how to spend their own development resources.

The result of this prioritization process was to generate considerable internal debate and not a little dissent about what were Level One and Level Two clients and how each should be treated. But having got to agreement in principle about the Levels, they were able to agree a way forward. Two partners were designated as Client Development Leaders for each of the 30 Level One prospects. In addition, ten other partners drawn from the best practices were assigned to each pair of Client Development Leaders to support their endeavours. By focusing on a few key prospects and the commitment of the right resources to them, the law firm was able to grow and it was also able to jettison less profitable clients. It became one of the fastest growing law firms in London.

The response to this myth is very simple but it is hard to effect. You first have to know who your right customers are; you then have to know what they most value; and then you have to deliver it to them. Then if the right customer complains because you are not treating them right, they are right to complain.

The right customer is always right.

Further reading

David Kean and Chris Cowpe, *How to Win Friends and Influence Profits*, Marshall Cavendish, 2008

YOU NEED MANY DECADES TO BUILD A TRULY GLOBAL BRAND

While we are witnessing global brands being built in shortening timeframes, this is quite a different thing from enduring and thriving over the long term.

This myth is more nuanced than it may first appear.

For a significant part of the past 100 years, building a global brand *did* take a considerable amount of time. Since the mid 1970s, though, things have been changing and today we find ourselves surrounded by global brands that in some instances took less than a decade to build.

Like the rest of the known, observable universe it seems that the process of brand building is speeding up.

It's not really possible to meaningfully probe this area without first trying to establish what we mean by a global brand. Many well-known brands might already see themselves as in some ways 'global' especially if they are easily accessible online and have at least some customers in different regions of the world. But when we talk about global brands we are really talking about those brands that have achieved incredibly high levels of recognition and are globally present (if not dominant) in all regions of the world. These brands are the giants, the behemoths of commerce and the brands that are seen by some as emblematic of all that is wrong with global capitalism.

For us, of course, these are the brands which have managed to serve more customer needs, more of the time, in more places and have generally done a better job at it than most of their competitors. They may now hold a dominant market position but that is usually a position that has been hard won.

A working definition of 'global brand'

A truly global brand can be identified thus:

- It is likely to be one of the largest brands operating in its category and very often will be part of one of the largest corporations in the world, with correspondingly huge revenues.
- It will have high levels of awareness, so whether you live in Tahiti or Tashkent you are likely to be familiar with it.
- It will be a brand that, irrespective of where it is headquartered, will earn significant revenues from nearly all of the major trading regions.

This definition is also the one that is broadly adhered to in Interbrand's league table – for anyone wanting to look at this in more detail you will find many of the brands referenced in this chapter included in that table.

So what are the global brands we are talking about? There are of course brands like Coca-Cola, Disney and McDonald's. Most people on a high street anywhere in the world would probably come up with a list of ten global brands as easily as they could count to ten. They are ubiquitous; they are so familiar in fact that they form part of the fabric of our everyday lives.

Yet it's not just consumer brands that have achieved this status. IBM, a business-to-business brand, regularly tops the global brand value league tables; in 2017 it achieved tenth position in Interbrand's 'Best Global Brands' study, with an estimated brand value in excess of $46 billion. Most people in the world are likely to have some idea about who IBM is and what it does. Not bad for a business brand that specializes in technology consultancy.

Some global brands have been around a long time

Let's start by acknowledging the reality that some of our biggest global brands did take a long time to build. A brand with unquestionably some of the highest levels of awareness on the planet is also one of the oldest, Coca-Cola. This brand was reputedly started on 29 January 1892, which makes it 126 years old. This brand began life in a small store and it is now a global corporation. Coca-Cola's journey has literally been the story of global capitalism.

Compared to Coca-Cola, oldies like Toyota and Samsung are relative newcomers, both having been founded about eighty years ago. The book *Established* lists a number of businesses that have been around for hundreds of years. They include Guinness (established 1759) and Wrigley (1886), both global brands. It is amazing to think about the journey these brands have been on. The global events and different market challenges that each would have had to overcome; the willingness, foresight and stamina to navigate each challenge; the inevitable mistakes that had to be endured and the lessons learnt. A bit like an established global music artist, many of these brands have developed and matured in the public eye, growing by finding ways to stay fresh, exciting and relevant to their customers. So if it has taken these giants of branding many decades to reach their ascendancy, perhaps these brands are actually grist to the myth?

Some tech brands are older than you think

This feeling might be further compounded when we tell you that some of our most celebrated technology brands are also a bit older than you might think. Apple, for example, was founded in Cupertino, California on 1 April 1976. That makes arguably the most valuable business in the world 42 years old. Not exactly an old person in human terms, but certainly within most people's definition of middle age. Of course brands are often long in gestation and it took the return of Steve Jobs in 1997 to really rekindle Apple's mojo and to turn Apple (along with its employees) into the business that it is today.

Interestingly Microsoft, Apple's long-time nemesis, was born just a year earlier, on 4 April 1975; even a brand as ubiquitous as Microsoft could not exactly be called a spring chicken.

So if it's taken the likes of Apple and Microsoft over forty years to become the dominant global players in personal computing (albeit in different ways), is it possible for any brand to do it more quickly? Jobs and Gates took their brands from their parents' garages to the top of the world. They mixed vision with incredible talent and entrepreneurialism to become the dominant forces in computing and connected smart devices. They saw different versions of the future and both were able to successfully achieve them. Could anyone beat these two?

The mythbusters

Even the achievements of Steve Jobs and Bill Gates are to some extent overshadowed – at least in velocity terms – by the incredible rise of Amazon and Facebook. These businesses are relative youngsters, Amazon having been founded just less than twenty-four years ago and Facebook at eighteen still in its teens! These businesses have gone from nowhere to being globally dominant in a quarter of the time it has taken Samsung to become a global brand. That is truly remarkable. Has anyone managed a higher velocity rate than Facebook? Well, both Netflix and PayPal are both (at the time of writing) still twenty, so as incredible as their rise has been even they don't quite beat Facebook.

Why has that been possible? In the case of Facebook it's the sheer power of technology to facilitate communication and social interaction. It has grown on the back of an explosion in connected smart devices. As these devices have grown cheaper and more accessible and because the mobile operators are not dependent on the fixed infrastructure that used to hold back developing countries, so more and more people have been able to get connected. Of course Facebook is also highly efficient. It requires a relatively small number of employees to administer this giant of social media. Some may argue that these brands are not truly global as they are restricted from operating in territories like China. Perhaps that is true in absolute terms, but the geographic reach of Facebook and its popularity across Asia is undeniable.

Amazon is in some ways even more remarkable. While it has undoubtedly been helped by all of the trends we have outlined above, it has also made huge investments in technology and physical infrastructure. Amazon made a huge bet on the future direction of retail and it looks as though it was right. Not only does Amazon have a huge business in the US but also it is present in over thirteen countries, including places like India where Prime is now available in more than 100 cities. The e-commerce potential of a country like India is huge. The sheer scale and complexity of Amazon's business are astonishing. And not only has it managed to continue building its core, it has successfully expanded into publishing, content distribution, TV production and broadcasting, smart devices and now intelligent voice-activated devices. Amazon has probably been helped by access to large amounts of relatively cheap capital and a patient investor community but it looks very much as though Amazon is getting its big bets right.

For anyone interested we urge you to read Jeff Bezos's letter on the difference between Day 1 companies and Day 2 companies (Chapter 10). It's fascinating stuff and it is his personal view on the mindset required to stay ahead. Needless to say it says a lot about the importance of staying close to your customer.

The arrivistes

However (and perhaps appropriately), Tesla has managed to usurp them all. Tesla is just coming up to its fifteenth birthday. A quite extraordinary feat, Tesla occupies No 98 in Interbrand's league table, with an estimated brand value of $4 billion. By virtue of its PR, its ambition and its (albeit not mass-market) revolutionary electric cars, Tesla has become a brand recognized by people across the world.

Brands like Uber and Airbnb are even younger. Uber is just nine years old and Airbnb is approaching its tenth birthday. While their rise has been spectacular both have recently encountered setbacks and neither has yet become a feature of top global brand league tables. It is great to be well known but a truly global brand also generates very significant global revenues. It will be interesting to see if and how long it takes them to leapfrog Lenovo and make it into the top 100.

A word of caution, though: while we are witnessing global brands being built in shortening timeframes, this is quite a different thing from enduring and thriving over the long term. Brands like Coca-Cola may have been created over a century ago but their achievement is to have been part of so many people's lives for so long. It will be fascinating to see how many of the more recent brands we have covered here will be around in the next twenty years.

It is true that for quite a big chunk of the last 100 years (and even beyond that) it took many decades to build a truly global brand. It has even taken a fast-moving and heavily franchised business like

McDonald's sixty-three years to reach the position of ascendancy that it occupies today. But times change and what was once a truism has now become something of a myth.

It is now quite obvious that it takes much less time to build a genuinely global brand. Tesla has managed to achieve global brand status in just a little less than fifteen years. It is also quite possible that this process will get even faster. Even if Uber or Airbnb don't manage it, here's betting that another brand will rise from relative obscurity and within just a handful of years become another global giant.

Further reading

Dark Angels, *Established: Lessons from the world's oldest companies*, Unbound, 2018

Interbrand, Best Global Brands 2017: http://interbrand.com/best-brands/best-global-brands/2017/ranking

A BRAND IS 'OWNED' BY THE MARKETING DEPARTMENT

The CEO has to ensure that the brand is intimately connected to the voice of the customer, that the business understands what customers need and that this is reflected in the way the customer journey is organized.

This myth is stubbornly persistent. The issue of ownership is more complex than it might first appear.

In a strict legal sense, the brand belongs to the entity or individuals that has ownership of the trademarks. In many instances the trademarks will be owned by the business that trades under them, but this is not always the case. Some businesses trade under licence, meaning they pay a third party for the privilege of being able to use their intangible assets, namely their trademarks and IP. This model is frequently used in the drinks industry, when a local manufacturer produces and brands drinks under licence from a third-party owner. In some instances (mostly to minimize their tax exposure), businesses will even license their brand back to their own local operating businesses. Brands are incredibly powerful and valuable assets and as such are usually held, procured or licensed centrally. They are rarely owned by the marketing department.

While it is true that a brand, by virtue of its trademarks and IP, can be legally owned, the really interesting thing about brands is that in two other significant ways, it is the customer who owns the brands. Firstly, as an intangible the brand actually exists and vests within the mind of the customer and secondly, due to a little-known legal concept called 'transference of rights', once a customer has bought a branded product, for example a Mars chocolate bar, at the moment of purchase the product actually becomes the property of the customer.

It is not unlike the Catholic understanding of transubstantiation: at the moment of communion, the wafer and wine become the *actual* body and blood of Christ. Similarly, at the point of purchase the brand becomes the property of the customer. Until they have consumed the product, and for as long thereafter as they care to believe it has an effect on their life, that very specific branded product belongs to them. And yet of course the intangible asset called the Mars brand remains the property of Mars Corporation, just as the intangible concept of God remains God's.

It's all about the customer

This distinction is important for several reasons. First, your brand is really just the sum of all of the things that you have ever said and done. As Jeff Bezos, CEO of Amazon reputedly remarked, a brand is 'what people say about you when you are not in the room'. It is the impression that you leave in the mind of your customer. Secondly, if you lose sight of what your customer wants then your brand is likely to quickly lose relevance and appeal. Thirdly, if your customer owns your brand then the CEO is the one who is now in charge of managing it.

Why marketing was perceived to own the brand

In the early days of post-war consumerism, brands were initially performing a badging and signposting function. They were a simple way of differentiating one product or service from that of another. Businesses didn't tend to pay huge amounts of attention to the intimate needs and requirements of their customers. A business typically made a product and then looked for ways to sell more of it. A product was made, badged and then depending on the size and resources of the company, advertised. In this context it is easy to see why businesses believed that the marketing department owned the brand; they were the ones branding the product and developing the messaging.

It wasn't really until the late 1960s and early 1970s that many businesses began to ask their customers what they actually wanted. This caused a lot of business angst and industrial turmoil. Suddenly markets were flooded with new and exciting products manufac-tured to reasonable quality levels at highly competitive prices. Entire industries were disrupted as new brands like Honda, Datsun and Sony were made available to an eager public. Over the subsequent decades marketing departments in most businesses became necessar-ily more sophisticated. They conducted qualitative and quantitative research, segmented and prioritized their customers, built a portfo-lio of brands and launched integrated campaigns across TV, radio, newspapers, direct and field marketing. Marketing was profession-alizing itself, reinforcing the sense that they 'owned' the brand; after all they had people called 'brand managers'.

At the same time businesses were also structured so that each department broadly mirrored their place on the value chain. Purchasing, engineering, production, finance, sales, marketing and human resourcing – all operating in their individual silos and getting their job done. Each owned its area of expertise. Of course in reality the brand still resided in the mind of the customer but it didn't *feel* like that. Perceptually and practically the brand still belonged to the marketing department.

Then in 1989 the internet was invented and the starting gun was fired on what was to eventually become the digital revolution. The growth in computing power, mobile technology, data transfer and convergence changed the world forever. Fast-forward to the present and we exist in a world where we can interact with brands in any way and via any medium we like. If we want to buy a product on our mobile phone and get it delivered the next day then we expect this to happen seamlessly. If we contact someone in customer services then we expect relevant people inside the business to be made aware of the issue and be on hand to quickly and speedily resolve it. When we revisit a retailer's website we expect it to remember what we were looking at last time or make helpful suggestions around what we might find new and interesting. If we want to hail a cab instantly or customize a product at the touch of the button then we have a reasonable expectation that this will happen. We live in a world where Amazon can deliver most of its inventory to our doors within twenty-four hours, where we can order a product from Argos at 5.30pm and have it delivered to our homes at 8.30pm, where we can transact with HSBC bank across a multitude of channels and devices and receive a fast, secure and seamless experience.

The changing role of the CEO

Of course, behind the scenes, giving customers the kind of seamless and fluid experiences they have come to expect is difficult and complex. It requires businesses to be joined up and responsive and to act coherently across all parts of the customer journey, to recognize that technology and the power of social media mean that brands can't afford to have a gap between what they say and what they do. In many markets businesses are now finally aligning and organizing around the customer – a physical acknowledgment that the brand is (and always was) owned by the customer and that the orchestration and delivery of the branded customer experience is now expected. The CEO has effectively become the senior brand manager.

The CEO has to ensure that the brand is intimately connected to the voice of the customer, that the business understands what customers need and that this is reflected in the way the customer journey is organized. As well as having an intimate understanding of the financials, a CEO needs to develop a suite of forward indicators, things that help to ensure continuing relevance and appeal.

Figure 2 Why it's *always* Day 1: Jeff Bezos' open letter

"Jeff, what does Day 2 look like?"

That's a question I just got at our recent all-hands meeting. I've been reminding people that it's Day 1 for a couple of decades. I work in an Amazon building named Day 1, and when I moved buildings, I took the name with me. I spend time thinking about this topic.

"Day 2 is stasis. Followed by irrelevance. Followed by excruciating, painful decline. Followed by death. And *that* is why it's *always* Day 1."

To be sure, this kind of decline would happen in extreme slow motion. An established company might harvest Day 2 for decades, but the final result would still come.

I'm interested in the question, how do you fend off Day 2? What are the techniques and tactics? How do you keep the vitality of Day 1, even inside a large organization?

Such a question can't have a simple answer. There will be many elements, multiple paths, and many traps. I don't know the whole answer, but I may know bits of it. Here's a starter pack of essentials for Day 1 defense: customer obsession, a skeptical view of proxies, the eager adoption of external trends, and high-velocity decision making.

Jeff Bezos, CEO of Amazon, has an interesting perspective on this challenge. He talks about the importance of always remaining a 'Day 1' company and not a 'Day 2' company. According to Bezos, 'Day 1' companies are intimately connected to their customers' needs and never stand still. They eschew proxies and are naturally cautious of relying solely on customer research – they take the time to speak directly to customers and understand the real issues behind the headlines. 'Day 2' companies are those who through their disinterest in the customer have already embarked on the process of decline, relying too much on research and benchmarking, too satisfied with their own performance. Bezos is particularly instructive for those CEOs seeking to understand the nature of their role in today's digitized economy.

A brand is what a brand does

The biggest single consequence of the digital revolution on business has been to shine a light on the conduct and behaviour of individual businesses. If you give customers consistently poor service it is likely that a lot of people, courtesy of social media, will hear about it very quickly. If you espouse a position publicly but then do something different behind the scenes, the chances are that customers will find you out. If you treat your staff badly it won't stay a secret for long: platforms like glassdoor.com allow anyone who signs up to read the anonymous postings of employees from every type of business imaginable.

Now more than ever a 'brand is what a brand does': the business and the brand are inseparable. This has made the internal culture of a business critically important. No system in the world can compensate for poor or disgruntled employees; good service comes from a desire and willingness to do the best for the customer. Almost every celebrated service brand has invested heavily in its internal culture. Southwest airlines, Virgin Trains, Metro Bank and First Direct all know that the way to get remarkable service is to create a fantastic culture. It is possible to quantify this too. The Service-Profit Chain has long demonstrated a proven link between a great culture, a great service and profitable, highly satisfied customers. First proposed as a theory of business management in a 1994 article in the *Harvard Business Review* by James L Heskett, Thomas Jones, Gary Loveman, W Earl Sasser and Leonard Schlesinger, it was later the subject of a book by Heskett, Sasser and Schlesinger and is now a highly influential concept in business. The link it establishes has profound implications for any CEO looking to build a successful and respected business.

This requirement isn't just about empowering frontline staff. Giving all employees a clear sense of the purpose and motivation that sit behind the business is a key part of developing a high-performing organization.

Structure matters

Organizational structure matters too because it has the potential to frustrate attempts at building seamless and frictionless customer interactions. Businesses can no longer comprise a series of individual departments; they need to get better at corralling multidisciplinary teams to serve the needs of the customer. Data and insight can't be allowed to languish with the analytics team. Customer service can't be held back by poor systems. Staff can't fail to take the initiative because they are waiting for approval. Sales can't be allowed to frustrate a loyal customer because they failed to recognize them when they logged in. Digitally native businesses start with an advantage but this can be squandered through poor management or leadership. Established businesses, by contrast, have to break down silos and inertia and learn to operate with purpose and pace.

A brand belongs to the customer

For businesses of all types, future success will depend on their ability to organize around the customer, to accept that reputation is earned and not cynically manipulated, to move from a tendency to command and control towards a more open and flexible way of working. To understand that while trademarks and IP can be legally owned by a business or individual, the real power of brands is that they reside in the mind of the customer and that every single action taken on behalf of a customer has the potential to add value and equity.

That is why a brand is not 'owned' by the marketing department.

Further reading

Harvard Business Review, 'The Service-Profit Chain': https://hbr.org/2008/07/putting-the-service-profit-chain-to-work

W Earl Sasser Jr, Leonard A Schlesinger, James L Heskett, *The Service-Profit Chain: How leading companies link profit and growth to loyalty, satisfaction and value*, Free Press, 1997

BRAND PURPOSE IS JUST CSR BY ANOTHER NAME

Genuine brand purpose is not about traditional corporate social responsibility. It is an organization's primary motivation, the reason the brand exists in the first place.

Brand purpose is one of those topics increasingly being talked about in boardrooms and at business schools. In fact, the idea of adopting a purpose appears to be in danger of becoming fashionable. This presents both an opportunity and a risk. The idea that businesses should be placing a greater emphasis on the reason 'why' they exist should be broadly welcomed, but as with many things that suddenly become the latest c-suite discussion topic, it is also in danger of being fundamentally misunderstood and potentially corrupted. Brand purpose is less to do with traditional corporate social responsibility (CSR), defined by the FT Lexicon as 'a business approach that contributes to sustainable development by delivering economic, social and environmental benefits for all stakeholders', and everything to do with running a sustainable and effective enterprise.

Brand purpose is becoming a hot topic because businesses are realizing that customers are not just interested in what a business does or how it maintains an edge over its competition. Increasingly, customers are also interested in why a business exists. What is the motivation that sits at the heart of the enterprise?

Meaning matters

In many economies customers are now faced with a plethora of choice. In any given product or service category, it is likely that several businesses will be competing for your attention and your money. Customers find it difficult to genuinely differentiate between providers and to know who to trust. There is also widespread public distrust in politics and big business. This 'trust' crisis means that customers are understandably placing a much greater emphasis on the authentic and are seeking brands which they perceive have real value and greater meaning than simply making money.

In 2017 Havas Group published the results of its biennial research (Meaningful Brands 2017); this research covers 1,500 global brands and garners the opinions of over 300,000 respondents globally. The research tracks and measures the different relationships that people have with brands and it has consistently and conclusively demonstrated that brands considered to be more meaningful by customers are able to generate more value for the business – typically increasing their share of wallet by nine times the average and outperforming the stock market average by 206 per cent.

Being clear about the 'why' is becoming an important business imperative. It demonstrates to customers and employees that there is more to your business than just the short-term pursuit of profit. It places your activity in a broader context and helps illustrate how you are building long-term sustainable value.

Of course, generating a profit and acting responsibly remain the essential prerequisites for any good business, but these are consequences, the things that flow from good business decisions and good governance. A purpose is something quite different; it is the unchanging motivation, the thing that can help you make effective decisions about what is right for your customers and your employees. A purpose is about much more than a single action or a specific CSR initiative. It is the reason behind why you do what you do. Hence it should influence all aspects of your behaviour and guide you in times of difficulty or uncertainty.

Purpose in action: Ikea, IBM, Google

Ikea is an example of a business that has developed and enacted a powerful purpose which influences all aspects of its business. Its commitment to create 'a better everyday life for as many people as possible' infuses every aspect of the way it operates and behaves. Its purpose is rooted in the notion that good design should be available to everyone. It is an open and democratic business that provides well-designed and affordable products within the context of an engaging and entertaining retail experience. It thinks hard about the customer experience and makes a virtue of the things that make it affordable in the first place, namely self-collection, self-assembly and long queues. The purpose is also in evidence in the way that Ikea recruits and rewards staff: today 45 per cent of its managers are female and pay is structured around employee needs rather than simply mirroring the prevailing market average. In terms of sustainability, Ikea also invests billions in the production of green energy – mitigating the negative environmental and social impact of its significant energy requirements. This is further evidence of the purpose in action helping to create a 'a better everyday life for as many people as possible'.

For over 100 years, IBM has been influenced and guided by the purpose its inspirational President, Thomas Watson, articulated, namely the creation of 'information technologies to benefit mankind'. IBM's adherence to and enactment of this idea has enabled them to lead and traverse huge changes in the way technology has been utilized. From calculating machines, through to supercomputers, business consulting and the concept of the 'smarter planet', IBM has managed to stay relevant and in most instances ahead of the competitive set.

Google's stated purpose is to 'organize the world's information and make it universally accessible and useful'. It is a focus that has driven the business since its inception and it has proved incredibly successful. While it is a lofty and (perhaps) worthy ambition it certainly wasn't formed out of a CSR initiative. It goes to the very core of what Google does and how it makes and creates shared value.

Some important businesses have clearly seen the value in espousing and enacting a clear purpose. It can act like an operating system, shaping and guiding behaviour across the whole business. As we shall see it can also be very helpful in times of crisis.

Purpose and doing the right thing

In *On Purpose*, there is a story that demonstrates how purpose drives decision-making in critical times. Back in October 2012 the eastern seaboard of the United States was visited by Hurricane Sandy – this was the hurricane that was described as the storm of the century. It caused 85 deaths, left 8 million people without power, made thousands homeless and caused widespread damage to property and infrastructure.

One of the interesting aspects of this disaster was how different businesses chose to respond to the unfolding tragedy, In the book the authors explain that American Apparel, the US clothing retailer, decided that the best way to help those customers ravaged by the storm (or as they described it 'bored by the storm') was to offer them a 20 per cent discount on all clothing for a time-restricted period of 36 hours. American Apparel effectively saw the storm as a retail opportunity.

Contrast this with the approach taken by the Duracell and Tide brands. Neither attempted to 'sell' to their customers. Instead

Duracell deployed a number of branded power generators that went directly into the communities worst affected. Similarly, Tide launched mobile laundry centres giving people the much-needed opportunity to wash the few clothes they had. Duracell and Tide resisted the opportunity to chase revenue and instead found ways to genuinely help customers and their communities.

These two brands are both owned by P&G (Procter & Gamble) which itself is a purpose-led business. 'P&G's purpose is to touch and improve more consumers' lives with more P&G brands and products every day.' In a time of uncertainty, these brands instinctively knew how to respond appropriately to the crisis, because they were influenced by a clear purpose. They didn't just try to help; they knew *how* to help.

Finding and articulating your purpose

So how do you build or articulate a purpose that can positively influence all aspects of your business? Well, contrary to the myth, you don't start by looking at how you can do 'good' or how you address the sustainability agenda (you should be doing these things anyway!). You begin by finding the things that have the potential to unite your customers and your employees. You must ask a simple question that can prompt a considerable amount of soul-searching: 'What is it that matters most to our customers and our employees?' If you can crack this, you will be well on your way towards uncovering your authentic purpose.

Potential sources of confusion

This is also where a lot of the confusion starts creeping in and why purpose is often mistakenly lumped together with 'doing good' or enacting worthy CSR initiatives. We are too used to hearing brands and businesses talk about what they want to do and how they want to do it. For example, they want 'to be the number one' or 'offer great returns to investors'. But we are less familiar with hearing brands express a genuine motivation, the thing that really unites their customers and staff. So when we are finally presented with something that is expressed in more emotional terms it might feel like a worthy sentiment more befitting of a place in a sustainability report. This is to miss the point entirely. Brands that have at their heart an authentic and relevant purpose are revealing the truth about the relationship between their customers, their staff and their stakeholders. They are revealing the recipe for how value is created as well the plan for how it can be sustained.

What matters most to your customers and employees?

Nissan realized that air quality was becoming one of the most fundamental global issues for customers and employees – and that it was time for the automotive sector to take action to reduce emissions and improve air quality. While vehicles are generally becoming cleaner and more efficient, technology now offers the realistic prospect of dramatically reducing emissions and then eventually removing them all together. The same also applies to serious road accidents. Technology has the capability to make cars much safer and reduce the number of accidents. Nissan has therefore made zero emissions and zero fatalities the cornerstone of its purpose: 'Advancing mobility towards a zero-emissions and zero-fatalities future on the roads'. This statement of intent is made credible both by its leading position in electric vehicles and its continuing investment in electric and autonomous vehicle technology, which (together with the other manufacturers) has the potential to deliver an emission-free, fatality-free world.

What matters most?

As *On Purpose* explains, Premier Inn is an example of another business that successfully identified what mattered most to its customers and employees. At first pass, Premier Inn's purpose might feel less ambitious than Nissan's, but in the context of their business (and what they can meaningfully influence) it is no less powerful. Premier Inn realized that what mattered most to their customers and their employees was simply helping customers to 'feel brilliant'. Most guests at a Premier Inn are usually there for a specific reason, often for an important business meeting or family event. What guests value most is being made to feel great so that they can go out and be the best version of who they are; employees in turn are motivated by helping guests feel great. 'Making their customers feel brilliant' has been adopted as the core purpose of the organization and it has directly influenced a powerful proposition, to give every customer a 'great night's sleep'. Investment has been focused on delivering against this proposition with the specific introduction of Hypnos beds and the upgrading of air conditioning across all rooms. Premier Inn isn't just in the business of being a hotel – it is in the business of making its guests feel brilliant.

An effective purpose has to be based on what matters most to *your* customers and employees. Sometimes (depending on the scale and reach of an organization) this will be an issue as big as global air quality but often, as with Premier Inn, it can be a more modest but no less authentic ambition based around the idea of making a guest 'feel brilliant'. Both matter. Each purpose is an authentic expression of why that organization exists.

A cautionary tale, the perils of purpose

Sometimes a brand takes the decision to clothe itself very publicly in the mantle of a worthy purpose or a fashionable cause. It makes that purpose the centre of its brand communications, even encapsulating it in a slogan or repeated copyline.

This can prove problematic if the business operations are not always 100 per cent aligned to it. Customers are increasingly sensitive to brands that profess to stand for one thing and then do something else completely incongruent with that. BP is a case in point. In 2000 the business embarked on a $200 million rebranding programme in which it sought to reposition itself as a green energy business, looking ultimately to move 'Beyond Petroleum' and become a sustainable energy company. Some commentators remained unconvinced, but many more saw BP as an enlightened business, trailblazing a new, more progressive approach to energy production. For a while BP really did seem as though it was making progress. It invested heavily in solar and wind energy and sought to bring safer domestic heating and cooking fuels and micro-energy to developing economies. Even its competitors began to emulate its approach. All of this was seriously challenged in April 2010 when a BP-operated rig exploded in the Gulf of Mexico and as a result a 'sea-floor gusher' flowed unchecked for 87 days. During that period Deepwater Horizon (as the disaster became known) released an estimated 4.9 million barrels of oil directly into the ocean.

Of course, drilling for oil is often a perilous and technically demanding activity and however professionally it is undertaken accidents will occur. But what aggravated an already grievous situation was the perceived initial reaction of the incumbent CEO Tony Hayward, who was criticized for not sufficiently acknowledging in public the full seriousness of the situation and who was reported as complaining that his holiday had been cut short by the crisis. After an extremely long period of time and several attempts the gusher was eventually capped and the oil finally contained.

Environmental impact aside, what hurt BP was the US Supreme Court in 2014 upholding earlier rulings that BP had been 'grossly negligent and guilty of wilful misconduct'. Transocean and Halliburton were also found to be partly culpable but the primary responsibility for the disaster was found to be BP's. The reason for the negligence was traced back to significant levels of underinvestment, which some interpreted as effectively sweating off the assets in order to maximize profits.

If an oil business makes the decision to move 'beyond petroleum' then this change has to be profound and invested in profoundly. It has to be something that the whole business is behind. It cannot profess to be green and make significant investments in (albeit heavily subsidized) sustainable technology on the one hand, while simultaneously being accused of underinvesting in its core business to the point of gross negligence, placing people's lives and the environment at risk on the other.

It is arguable that its reputational damage was greater because its 'green conversion' was so painfully and publically undermined. It is a particularly acute example of what happens when an initiative or proposition is elevated to that of an organizational purpose without the entire business relentlessly focused on it. Perhaps for understandable reasons, BP has retreated from its overtly green positioning. This disaster has so far cost BP billions of dollars. A less resilient business would probably have folded.

Beware the metaphor

Uber is interesting because it professes to want to 'make transportation as reliable as running water, everywhere, for everyone'. At first glance this might seem like an honestly held motivation. Increasingly though, it feels more akin to an elegant business metaphor. There is no doubt that customers love Uber's convenience, but do the drivers and employees join for the same reason? Is this the thing that matters most to both customers and employees? What really unites these groups? Is the lack of a clear purpose and a creeping sense that Uber is chasing commercial gain at any cost beginning to impact negatively on Uber's growth?

By 2018 Uber was beset by a whole host of problems, many of which can arguably be traced back to culture and issues with corporate governance. Its founder and CEO; Travis Kalanick, has had to resign (although he retains a seat on the board) amid a sexual harassment scandal and reports of senior executives visiting escort bars in South Korea. Police in the UK have accused Uber of not reporting sex attacks by drivers. The Mayor of London has revoked (and temporarily restored) Uber's operating licence, citing concerns over passenger safety and corporate governance. The business is similarly being challenged in a host of other jurisdictions. Uber has also been accused of spying on customers and is embroiled in disputes about the legal status of its drivers. Many of these issues seem symptomatic of a business that has adopted an elegant metaphor rather than an authentic purpose. It's an example of what happens when a business pursues growth at any cost.

Power of purpose

A genuine brand purpose is not about traditional corporate and social responsibility. It is the authentic expression and enactment of an organization's primary motivation, the reason why that brand or business exists in the first place, often found in the one thing that matters most to both customers and employees.

As we have seen, a brand purpose can be a powerful source of inspiration and guidance. It can help build meaningful relationships with customers and employees and unlock sustainable value for your business. But beware pretenders. Businesses that fail to embrace a genuine motivation, or worse seek to align themselves with a fashionable cause that they don't really believe in, may find themselves undone. In business as in everyday life, your deeds matter as much as your words.

Further reading

Shaun Smith and Andy Milligan, *On Purpose: How to deliver a branded customer experience people love*, Kogan Page, 2015

Meaningful Brands 2017: https://havasmedia.com/meaningful-brands-reap-greater-financial-rewards/

What Uber's troubles tell us about the importance of company values: www.ft.com/content/95cebf4a-76d7-11e7-a3e8-60495fe6ca71

MYTH 12

CUSTOMERS ARE SEEKING A PERSONAL RELATIONSHIP WITH YOUR BRAND

Irrespective of how appealing and engaging you are, most customers are not actively seeking a relationship with you.

It is not that surprising that brands often see their primary responsibility as building deep and continuing relationships with customers. Indeed, practitioners often talk about the importance of building valuable relationships and a whole industry, customer relationship marketing (CRM), has grown up around the idea that the majority of customers are seeking some kind of personal relationship with their favourite brands. As convincing as all this may sound it is largely a myth.

Don't assume you have permission to start a relationship

Let's start with the idea of a personal relationship. While you may identify with, engage with, and enjoy the company of many people, you will have a much smaller set of people that you would describe as being intimately connected with. The same applies to brands. While you might identify with a brand, engage with a brand and even value a brand, you are (in most instances) unlikely to be seeking an actual relationship with that brand. You may respond emotionally to a brand but that isn't necessarily the same thing as wanting a deep personal relationship. The power of a brand vests in its ability to build an emotional connection but (as in many aspects of life) we shouldn't automatically assume that this means it has permission to start a relationship.

The evidence backs this up too. In 2012 the *Harvard Business Review* published an article, 'Three myths about what customers want', in which they warned practitioners to be wary of the idea that customers are seeking relationships with brands. After running a study with 7000 consumers they found just 23 per cent of those surveyed described themselves as being in a relationship with a brand. The majority, 77 per cent, didn't actually perceive themselves as being in a relationship with any brand. Interestingly when the majority were asked why, they typically responded with comments like: 'It's just a brand, not a member of my family.' So while a significant minority of customers are open to a relationship (and we will explore this later) the majority, it turns out, are not.

So what are the implications of this? Fundamentally that we should be wary of overstating the amount of time and attention that brands occupy in our consciousness. This does not mean that brands can't occupy a valuable piece of mental real estate in the minds of customers, but we should be realistic about the time customers are likely to spend contemplating their relationship (or indeed the relative differences) between brands. Instead of bombarding customers with hundreds of emails that attempt to infer a relationship that most likely doesn't exist, focus instead on making your brand distinctive and engaging. As Deloitte stated in their July 2017 Consumer Review: 'Winning and retaining customers in the digital era requires a mix of personalization, relevance, exclusivity and engagement across all the different channels.'

That said; we should not forget the opportunity afforded by the 23 per cent of customers that are open to a relationship. These customers are likely to be highly engaged and particularly responsive to brands that are perceived as meaningful or purpose-led. Customers in this group have the propensity to become good customers, passionate brand advocates and valuable super-users. Nonetheless, we should not make the mistake of assuming that the majority of customers want a personal relationship with a brand; most customers simply want to be engaged, recognized and incentivized.

Customers may not want a conversation with you

As well as having a healthy scepticism for the idea that customers want a relationship with your brand, you should be similarly suspicious about the idea that your customers want a conversation with you. Most do not. This misunderstanding probably contributes significantly to the erroneous idea that most customers are seeking some kind of relationship. There will be times when customers want to talk directly to brands, but on the whole this will be to notify the brand or operator that something has gone wrong. It is vital to provide your customers with different ways of contacting you and it is very important that you listen, take appropriate action and don't attempt to muzzle legitimate complaint. But don't confuse these situations with a desire to start an actual conversation. Customers generally want brands to quickly and efficiently remedy any lapse in service and remediate any financial loss. In these circumstances they will usually find attempts to start a 'conversation' both patronizing and irritating.

The truth is that most customers would rather talk to each other. Most people don't want to have a conversation with a 'brand'.

They want to talk to other people who share the same values, beliefs or interests as they do. Ergo, the most influential communities that surround some of our best-known brands often comprise fiercely independently minded individuals who are hugely passionate about either the brand itself or the activity to which it is connected. PlayStation and Harley-Davidson are two brands with very active communities. PlayStation provides an online space for gamers to connect. They have made it easy for users to home in on their specific interests or to find help and support. The site supports the creation of user-generated content and PS4 users can upload in-game clips directly online. The community is linked to PlayStation's social media channels on YouTube and Twitter, allowing content to be shared by gamers, developers and key titles. Harley-Davidson has been supporting the development of its community (Harley Owners Group) since the 1980s. It reportedly has over a million members and is a community centred on a shared passion and lifestyle.

Help your supporters talk to each other

These brands have realized that their role is to propagate and support a community rather than try to dominate it. They occasionally post content and updates but otherwise leave the community to thrive and develop. Some of the most influential and useful online communities are unofficial communities like this. Lugnet, for example, is one of the largest unofficial communities of Lego fans, comprising mostly adults who build complex Lego projects and share their work. Lego has acknowledged its role as a valuable source of information and insight.

Starbucks has supported an online community, called My Starbucks Idea, and in effect engineered the creation of a global suggestion box. It encourages ideas and suggestions from the 150,000-plus community members on how to improve the customer experience. It then implements what it perceives as the best ideas.

Customers can be incredibly passionate about their favourite brands, but this passion should not be misinterpreted as a signal that they are looking for a personal relationship. Most are not.

Customers may be less loyal than you think

For a long time it was assumed that loyalty programmes were great ways of building meaningful relationships with customers. As data collection and analysis became more sophisticated, brands like Tesco were able to use this data to offer groups of customers' highly targeted coupons and incentives. Not only did Tesco attribute much of its stellar growth to the success of its Clubcard programme, the belief was that Tesco had built strong and enduring personal relationships and had effectively 'locked-in' customers. Then came the 2008 financial crisis and shoppers' habits quickly began to change. It turned out that for the ordinary 'cash-strapped' shopper what mattered most in their decision about where to shop was the price they paid at the till. Shoppers quickly changed their habits. They started shopping more frequently and while they would still treat themselves to the occasional indulgence, shoppers were now sourcing the majority of their everyday items as cheaply as possible. Retailers like Tesco quickly discovered that in the midst of a downturn their customers were less sticky than they had thought.

Of course, as loyalty programmes became more ubiquitous and possibly less generous, their power undoubtedly diminished (to the point where many have become tedious), but this also serves to illustrate the wider point that customers are perhaps more promiscuous than practitioners would care to admit.

Use the right tools for the right kind of customer

As a consequence of all this, there is now a lot of debate about the value and usefulness of running a loyalty programme. Many commentators feel it is difficult to justify the investment of such a programme (at least on the basis of a straight financial return) when money might be more effectively spent elsewhere. The logic is not to spend money trying to make customers committed; rather, you should keep them interested, engaged and incentivized.

The same applies to the use of email marketing. There is little doubt that email can be a highly effective sales tool but it needs to be used sparingly. A customer might well be interested in the occasional targeted sales promotion, but on the basis that they are probably not seeking a relationship with you, don't bombard them with unwanted chatter and daily incentives – these activities are likely to be irritating as well as potentially damaging to your longer-term brand equity.

Of course, we know that there are a minority of customers who don't mind being in a relationship. These customers can be nurtured and treated differently (especially in high-value, high-status categories). But it's important to remember that irrespective of how appealing and engaging you are, most customers are not actively seeking a relationship with you.

There is good news, though. Once you fully embrace this reality you can become a much more effective practitioner. Once you have identified the different types of customer, you can start treating them in ways that are likely to elicit a better and more valuable response. You can build a deeper discourse with the minority of customers who are seeking a relationship with you and harness their power as brand advocates and future community leaders. You can invite them to insider events, reward their affinity and recognize their role as a source of insight and inspiration. Burberry does this very effectively. It has a well-deserved reputation for making its brand more accessible and easier to interact with. Customers who are highly committed to the brand or people who are seen as important influencers or celebrities are regularly invited to catwalk shows and other VIP events. These events provide opportunities to build engagement and associate Burberry with glamour and prestige.

The mobile network giffgaff has taken this idea a step further and created a network effectively run by its community of customers. At giffgaff the customers are the customer services team; as well as solving a range of day-to-day problems, the community is consulted on a range of issues including potentially sensitive subjects, such as price rises. As customers are effectively responsible for managing the first tier of customer service, things are dealt with quickly and efficiently. Additionally, as the business is operating with a relatively small overhead, customer pricing can then be kept as low as possible. Not all customers will be active participants in the community, but the business is making efficient use of those who want to be.

Harvest the benefits of being more realistic

So what about the majority of customers who may find you appealing and engaging but who are not necessarily seeking a personal relationship with you? Well, the good news is that you can stop wasting your time trying to build a deeper relationship with them and devote your resources to becoming more relevant and appealing. We believe that modern practitioners have always tended to overestimate the role that their brand plays in the lives of their customers. Once this is recalibrated and a more realistic view taken on the nature of the relationship we are seeking with brands, then the practitioner is liberated from the constraints of the past.

Importantly this liberation shouldn't just be interpreted as a quest for transactional ease. We aren't advocating a race to bottom, where brands compete solely on the basis of price or how easy they are to interact with. Being easy to find and easy to do business with are undoubtedly important but it is unlikely to be a long-term source of competitive advantage. Just because the majority of customers do not want to be in a relationship with us, it does not absolve us of the need to be interesting, engaging and relevant.

While the tools and techniques used to build brands have undoubtedly changed, the basic appeal of a brand has not. A brand works because it is able to establish a mix of emotional and rational associations that exist wholly in the mind of the customer; these distinctive and sometimes unique associations help to differentiate the goods and services of one undertaking from that of another. Brands are valuable because they are difficult to copy, they help to generate demand and they can help support an enhanced price position.

Stay ahead of your customers' needs and motivations

Practitioners should keep in mind that as well as minimizing the pain for the customer, part of their job is also to maximize customers' utility and enjoyment. A brand needs to work hard to maintain its relevance and it needs to ensure that it is always keeping up with (if not ahead of) its customers. Customers' needs and motivations constantly change and understanding how these shift is critical to staying ahead. This is particularly important when we already know that most customers are reluctant to become too intimate, even with the brands they really like. Thus investing in and acting upon genuine insight become very important. A brand may find that it is struggling not because of ease or availability but because it is not aligned to customers' changing needs or motivations. Who knew that customers would be persuaded to buy a computer based on how it looked rather than how it performed? Steve Jobs did. He realized that there were motivations and requirements not being satisfied by the status quo. Who realized that customers' faith in air travel was sufficiently established to presage and facilitate the arrival and growth of the low-cost operator? Southwest Airlines did. Who spotted that the men's razor category was out of ideas? Dollarshave Club did and as a consequence of their entertaining and disruptive approach they finished up being bought by Unilever for $1 billion.

The danger of ignoring changing needs and motivations is clear for all to see. M&S Clothing, Mothercare and House of Fraser are all examples of brands struggling to stay relevant. Brands that are perceived as 'stuck in the middle', offering middling products at middling stores for middling prices are in trouble. These brands will continue to struggle until they better understand and act upon the needs and motivations of their shoppers. No amount of store closures and retrenchment alone will be sufficient to address the problem; an imaginative and informed approach is required.

Be wary of the idea that the majority of customers are seeking a personal relationship with your brand; most of them are not. Recognize this and you can start to build a more effective brand. Nurture the smaller cohort of customers who are open to a relationship and help them to build a community where customers can talk openly to each other. Use the money you would have spent trying to build relationships with customers who aren't interested, to sharpen your offer, build distinctiveness and use insight to stay with and ahead of changing customer needs and motivations. By all means make things easy for your customers but don't assume that's all you need to do.

Further reading

Clive Humby and Terry Hunt, *Scoring Points*, 2008
Harvard Business Review, Three myths about what customers want,
    2012: https://hbr.org/2012/05/three-myths-about-customer-eng
Deloitte Consumer Review 2017: www2.deloitte.com/content/dam/
    Deloitte/uk/Documents/consumer-business/deloitte-uk-consumer-review-
    customer-loyalty.pdf

BRANDING IS SUBJECTIVE. IT'S ALL FLUFF AND ART WITH NO RIGOUR AND SCIENCE

There are tools to guide the practitioner and to provide shortcuts but they should never replace the human factor that sits at the heart of every successful brand.

Today's budding marketer has access to a huge range of literature, online content and academic research. Marketing is very much an established discipline and consequently it has all of the attendant trappings: luminaries, textbooks, university degrees, professors and even its own professional body. This is not quite the case for the budding brand practitioner. John Murphy, the founder of Interbrand and self-styled 'Brandfather', recently asserted that branding, the structured discipline of creating and managing brands, was only invented in the 1970s, and arguably the notion of branding as a specialist discipline requiring its own specific support only became established over the past few decades. In addition, some of the tools created during this period have been rendered less effective as technology continues to disrupt and profoundly change the way we interact with the world and live our lives. So while there are effective processes and tools to help the brand practitioner there is generally less consensus about what is useful and where they can be found.

The truth is that there are far less accredited, approved or independently verified tools in branding than you will find in marketing. Indeed, the professional services firms with their centuries of qualifications and accrediting bodies tend to look at branding as a sort of pseudo-science and see brand agencies as sellers of emperor's new clothes or snake oil, putting unnecessary jargon around obvious concepts. This isn't fair. There are some really useful, practical and helpful tools at your disposal, developed by some fantastic practitioners who understand that building brands requires intelligence, creativity and imagination. Hopefully the next few pages will demonstrate that it's not all made up over a chai latte.

Some important distinctions

Before we examine this myth in any more detail, it is probably helpful to make the following points.

a) Marketing and branding are certainly linked activities but they are different in their orientation. Marketing is generally concerned with the selling of specific products and services while branding is concerned with the process of building an ownable space in the mind of the customer.

b) We make a distinction between two main types of brand, product brands typically found in FCMG (fast-moving consumer goods) categories (eg cereals or shampoo) and corporate and/or service brands (eg Microsoft or Virgin).

These distinctions are important because marketing and branding are terms that are often used interchangeably, when they are in fact separate disciplines; and the processes and tools specifically connected with product brands have a different history than those more readily associated with corporate or service brands.

The rise of the specialist brand agency

For a considerable part of the 20th century, the process of brand building was handled by the ad agency. Big brands tended to vest their business for long periods of time with the same agencies, and as a consequence they became (along with the client) the default 'owner' of the brand. A brand would typically be built through a series of individual campaigns, with the agency being responsible both for an authentic expression of the brand as well as the development of compelling and effective advertising.

The fictional but extremely well-researched series *Mad Men* provides a fascinating insight into this era. The ad agencies were under constant pressure to produce something interesting and distinctive for their clients. As a consequence they often sacrificed the evolving narrative arc of long-term brand development on the altar of short-term expediency. In addition, much of the advertising of this era was focused on selling the products of a booming post-war consumerist society – anything from cigarettes to cars.

Then towards the end of the 1970s, especially in the US and UK, we saw the emergence of the neo-liberal orthodoxy. Markets started to be privatized and deregulated, new corporations were formed and the service economy started to take hold. Suddenly there was a need for new brands to be created across a multitude of different sectors and this period marked the emergence of the specialist brand agencies. Things that were previously 'covered' by the ad agency, eg brand name development, brand architecture, brand positioning and brand narrative, were now taken over by a new breed of specialist agency who saw the benefits and opportunities that specialization would bring.

A few of these specialist agencies would effectively formalize or invent the processes required for disciplined and long-term brand creation and development. A little later these agencies would be joined by a host of design businesses, some of which could now add the strategic services they had previously lacked.

The invention of a new suite of tools

Each of these agencies had different levels of capability and each was involved in developing or refining their own tools and methods. Many of the agencies focused on brand positioning and design and they often simply co-opted versions of the models used by their large multinational clients. These multinational brand owners had been developing product brands for many years and as a result they were often seen as the definitive repositories for things like positioning tools. Unilever was a good example of this and variations of its tools (like the Brand Key) were widespread. Other agencies took their inspiration from different places, but over time a general consensus began to emerge around the best models and approaches to deploy.

Agencies that focused on corporate and service brands created tools that they believed were more suited to their specific challenges. Tools and approaches were developed for every aspect of the brand creation and development process.

Specific processes were created for developing brand names and agencies created new positioning tools. A method for determining the value of a brand was created and it was quickly joined by a number of competing methodologies, these slowly gaining credibility and support from within the finance community. Other agencies built tools for collecting insight or identifying opportunity areas. Brand architecture (the different ways of organizing a branded portfolio), became a discipline in its own right; experts in the field emerged, like David Aaker, who began to structure and formalize thinking around this topic. Agencies ultimately competed with each other to develop the best proprietary tools and proudly asserted and protected their proprietary thinking. This led to the creation of lots of helpful process and tools but each agency tended to have its own approach and its own glossary of terms. Standardization has been slow to emerge and thinking has often stayed inside businesses.

As a consequence there are fewer branding textbooks and university or MBA courses than you will find in related disciplines like marketing. But nevertheless there are some books, which contain some great help and advice for the practitioner. So in order to help the reader we will attempt to set out several of the fundamental branding tools that we perceive as critical to any brand development process and at the end of the chapter we will recommend the books that we think will be most helpful for those wishing to extend their knowledge and understanding.

The need for a definitive model

A legacy of the lack of standardization can still be felt today: there is still little consensus around what exactly constitutes the essential components of a brand as well as a lack of clarity around the terms used to describe them. Too many practitioners still omit important components altogether or else use loose or inaccurate terms to describe what they are trying to achieve. This can make things confusing and at times it can actively prohibit progress. For any practitioner requiring help on the fundamentals, take a look at our

Figure 3   Brand DNA model

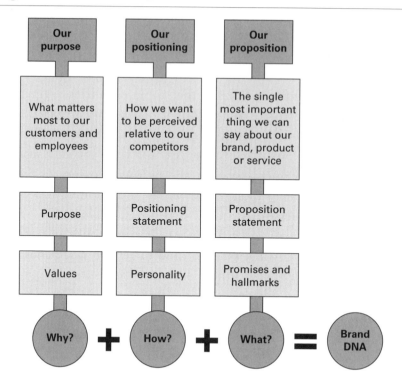

Brand DNA model. It contains what we believe are the essential components of any brand definition or development exercise.

Brand DNA

Brand purpose

The reason why a brand exists, an expression of its ultimate motivation.

Brand positioning

How the brand wishes to be perceived in its market relative to the competition.

Brand proposition

What the brand promises in order to create value, the single most important thing that can be said about the brand, product or service to the customer.

Brand promises and hallmarks

The explicit commitments, actions or behaviours that are given to customers in order to reflect the brand's intent.

Brand values

The brand's fundamental principles that shape its culture.

To add a little more explanation, the purpose is best thought of as the north star, an immutable guiding principle that, once articulated, should rarely change. As we mention in an earlier chapter, a purpose will most often be found by looking at what genuinely matters most to both customers and employees. A positioning will most likely evolve over time in response to the competitive context and should be something that can be inferred as opposed to being explicitly stated. A proposition, by contrast, may be regularly updated to reflect changing customer preferences or a different market dynamic. The promises are best thought of as distinctive product and service hallmarks. Brand values, once defined, should by their definition rarely change at all. Get these elements right and you will be a significant way towards building a compelling and motivating brand.

But a model (however good) is just a model. How do you ensure that you are populating the model with the right content and building something that when taken as a whole will be both compelling and distinctive for the customer? Aside from hard work, we believe that any process must start with a full understanding of the brand's situation. The practitioner must have a

Figure 4 4Cs audit model

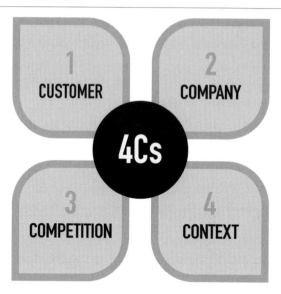

thorough appreciation of the overall context in order to understand how to develop the brand. We believe it is helpful to structure this initial groundwork and have developed a model to assist in the process – we call it the 4Cs analysis. Using this tool, the practitioner is required to look specifically at: the Customer, the Competition, the Company and the Context. Let's briefly explore each of these dimensions.

The 4Cs analysis tool

Customer

The way to maximize your chances of building a compelling brand is to build it on customer insight. A customer insight is an observation about the customer that can be acted upon. Some very successful brands have been founded on the basis of one very big insight. Anita Roddick founded The Body Shop on a big insight. She realized back in the late 1970s that customers were becoming more environmentally-conscious and that, importantly, those wanting to buy ethical cosmetics were being poorly served. Roddick launched a business to fill this gap and went on to build a highly successful ethical retail brand. Other brands have been built by executing against a series of smaller (but no less important insights). Spotify was not the first music streaming service, but by understanding the different ways in which customers enjoy music it has been able to build class-leading functionality, different levels of tiered access, high-resolution streaming services and seamless multi-device functionality. By understanding and acting upon what customers want they have been able to succeed by building a better mousetrap. The job of the brand practitioner is to take the time to really understand what you think the customer wants from your product or service. Importantly, customers don't always know what they want; very often the job of the practitioner is to spot what isn't being explicitly communicated and reading between the lines to extract genuine insight.

Qualitative and quantitative research methods are well known and can be useful tools in the practitioners' toolbox but other methods for garnering insight are increasingly being used. Large-scale data analysis can reveal new or previously unseen patterns of behaviour. Ethnographic research can help the practitioner literally immerse themselves in their customers' lives. Sophisticated web tools can search for opinion and sentiment and very often identify the precise activities that are shaping either a category or specific brand perceptions. It should also be remembered that in many sectors a company's employees, distributors and partners all have the potential to act as 'expert witnesses' and unlock customer insight.

Competition

To build a compelling brand you generally have to have a good idea of what your competitors are doing. Whether you are creating a brand from scratch or looking to reposition an existing one, it is important to know where there are valuable and potentially under-served opportunities. Sometimes it will be obvious where the positioning territories are; sometimes it will be less obvious and more nuanced. Occasionally there are opportunities to completely reframe the competitive landscape. Perhaps, like supermarket Lidl, you realize that while the traditional food retailers are offering a trade-off between choice, price and quality you can completely disrupt the model by restricting choice and instead offer great quality and incredibly low prices? Perhaps you don't see a single competitor as your enemy and instead you decide to invent one. Reebok famously did this with its iconic ad 'Belly's gonna get you!' Apple, Coke and Subaru have variously challenged totalitarianism, disharmony and mediocrity. We didn't know these were the enemies until these brands told us they were. When considering the competitive set it is also a good idea to consider both direct and indirect competitors. Did TomTom realize that its biggest competitors would turn out not to be other satnav manufacturers but Google and Apple? Did the private taxi business Addison Lee initially see a mobile-enabled app called Uber as a serious competitor?

Company

Most brand owners don't take long enough to think about both their real and perceived strengths. What is it that is genuinely different or unique about their brand and is this uniqueness being effectively utilized? We make the distinction between 'real' and 'perceived' because occasionally brands are ascribed leadership for facets that are not always class leading. We assume that Intel is a better class of chip than other manufacturers but most customers don't actually know they are. By successfully branding their chips customers have come to believe that their performance is universally better. We assume that brands like Audi and BMW are full of superior engineering but do we actually know whether they are (or are not) less reliable than their far-eastern counterparts? Knowing your real and perceived strengths gives you a real insight into what your customers think and provides a genuine foundation for any future positioning or proposition.

Context

This is about understanding the macro and micro trends influencing the sectors in which you operate. For an automotive manufacturer increasing levels of concern about air quality are likely to impact its sector and its business. For a coffee chain or supermarket, increasing concerns about the level of plastics entering our environment and polluting our water are likely to have a direct impact on customer sentiment and eventually the importance given to fully recyclable materials. Similarly, our love of ease may have ramifications for retail businesses, or if you are a bank you have to deal with the challenges posed by the fast-evolving block-chain technologies. It is not always possible to foresee every trend but thinking deeply about the wider context often reveals what your customers are or will be really interested in and worried about.

Context operates at the micro level too. What is happening within your sector may have a direct impact on how you choose to position your brand. For example, is new technology driving the development of your sector and if so are you best placed to lead on this? Are customers placing a greater value on freedom and flexibility and if so are you best placed to lead on this? The UK energy market is becoming more competitive and price sensitive; if you are a fledgling new entrant how do you meet this challenge? Do you seek a price leadership position or do you seek to build a different kind of sustainable advantage?

A thorough understanding of each of the 4Cs will give you a comprehensive foundation on which to build or develop your brand. A distillation may also help you identify a sweet spot, a rewarding territory on which to build your brand. Importantly, though, this model is not a replacement for the hard work and creative thinking that must accompany any brand-building activity. You will need to identify genuine insight, a tangible positioning space, real capability and a thorough understanding of the forces impacting upon or influencing your sector.

So now that we have identified a definitive brand model and explained a little about the groundwork needed to help you create or develop your brand, it is probably worth highlighting some of the other branding processes and where you can go to find out more about them.

Brand naming

Creating a brand name is still an essentially creative exercise, but there are many things to consider if you want to do it properly. It is often helpful to start by looking at the usefulness of the trademarks you already own, before definitively embarking on the quest for a new name. It is also helpful to have a reasonable idea of the type of name you want. For example, do you want a purely abstract name like Diageo which will be easier to create but expensive to build? Do you want something more associative like Uber or alternatively something much more descriptive (but potentially difficult to register) like comparethemarket.com? (One of the reasons the famous Compare the Meerkat advertising campaign was devised for this brand was precisely to help customers differentiate it from other similarly named competing businesses such as Go Compare). Once you are clear about the type of name you want to create then make sure you are clear about what trademark classes and territories you will be seeking to register your name in, as well as the process you will follow for creating a viable shortlist and undertaking the necessary searches and linguistic/cultural checks. Of course if you are a small brand just starting out in a single territory you will approach this differently from a large multinational brand owner operating in multiple jurisdictions, but many of the initial questions posed here are useful to think about.

Brand naming has not fundamentally changed as a process since John Murphy codified it in the early 1980s. You can find excellent chapters on the subject in a number of books, including *Trade Marks* and *Brand Strategy* (see Further reading).

Brand architecture

Depending on the situation and number of brands involved, creating an optimum portfolio of brands can be a complex endeavour – at the same time it is frequently overcomplicated and misunderstood. Brand architecture is really about finding the optimum way of structuring a portfolio of brands. Most of the time the job of a brand architecture is to make it easy for a customer to navigate the totality of what's on offer. When I buy a bar of Toblerone, for example, I am likely to be unconcerned or even unaware that it is ultimately owned by the American conglomerate Kraft. As a consequence, Toblerone receives a very light on-pack endorsement from its owner.

When I buy a car I am often much more interested in who the manufacturer is and consequently there is often a more obvious connection between the manufacturer and the model of car under consideration. BMW, Mercedes and Ford all major on the parent brand and use numbers or names to help customers navigate the ranges. Often a brand owner will use a range of brands within a portfolio to delineate price or different levels of experience. VW sells a range of cars under its own brand but it also sells premium vehicles under the Audi brand and cheaper vehicles under the Skoda brand. Often a new brand is required when the entry into a new market or new price point stretches the credibility of the existing brand too far.

Conversely, sometimes architecture is deliberately deployed to help build the corporate brand. Unilever is using its product brands to help build its corporate brand because it felt it was important to increase corporate transparency and sustainability. Architecture gets complicated because sometimes decisions need to be made about which brands to divest and which to keep or evolve and in other instances owners are constrained by historic associations or things peculiar to one specific market.

For further information about brand architecture we recommend the chapter in *Don't Mess with the Logo*, and you will find an excellent chapter on the subject in *Advanced Brand Management*.

Brand management

A difficult subject to capture in just a few paragraphs, brand management is about sustaining a distinctive and relevant offer, such that it stimulates demand and sustains loyalty. Brand management necessitates that you are measuring your brand performance over time using salient and helpful indicators. While we recognize the value that can be derived from tracking studies, we would also pay close attention to leading indicators, things that help you be predictive – customer conversations, advocacy scores, promoter scores, brand recognition and sentiment. As brands are primarily judged on what they do, it is important to be able to see and predict the commercial consequences of any changes that are made.

Brand valuation

A number of businesses offer methodologies and tools for valuing brands and taking a valuation-led approach to the management of a brand or branded portfolio. While many of these approaches are financially robust, nearly all involve some element of subjective opinion or assessment. In practice it is often difficult to divorce the pure contribution of brand from the rest of the business and so the final number is probably best regarded as indicative of the relative value of the brand rather than an absolute number. Nevertheless brand valuation is recognized by the accounting profession and is used to help determine things such as royalty rates and the price that should be paid for the brand as part of an acquisition or merger.

Whatever your view on the precise merits of brand valuation, nearly all of the associated methodologies involve some assessment of both *a*) the role of brand and *b*) brand strength. Role of brand attempts to determine the relative importance of a brand in any given category. For example, the role of brand in petrol retailing is relatively low but much higher in categories like luxury clothing and apparel. Brand strength attempts to look at how well-managed your brand is and therefore how likely it is to survive into the medium term. For example, a brand like Coca-Cola is likely to be extremely well managed and will therefore be highly likely to generate future healthy returns.

Of the two elements central to the methodology, we believe the most useful is brand strength. Most brand owners struggle to create an objective tool for the active measurement of their brand performance, but brand strength can be used as an objective framework across categories and geographies. It can comprise a mixture of indicators and is particularly useful for brand owners managing more complex portfolios.

Brand experience

As we reference in other chapters, brands are everything to do with the experiences they offer to their customers. If management tends towards measurement then measuring the customer experience and its impact on preference and loyalty is a good way of ensuring active management of the brand. Of course, in categories where the role of brand is considered to be very high, it is likely that the brand will have a greater sphere of influence in terms of its ability to shape behaviour and delivery, but as we have seen all businesses are increasingly measured on their ability to achieve high levels of organizational coherence.

Delivering a distinctive, appealing and memorable customer experience involves making decisions about what to prioritize. It necessitates a thorough understanding of your customer and the willingness to align investment behind the key touchpoints. easyJet is an example of a business that has made a clear decision to automate its booking and check-in processes and to make these as friction-free as possible. The mobile app makes it possible to manage all aspects of your journey; it keeps you updated and alerts you early if there are any problems with your flight. At Gatwick the bag drop process is almost entirely automated; consequently check-in is less stressful and queues are shorter. As well as being a good experience, all of this is congruent with easyJet's positioning as a low-cost carrier. As a satisfied customer, I simply don't care that I have to do much of the legwork.

Brand experience is a big subject but for those seeking a definitive perspective on how to create a great customer experience we would point you in the direction of the Harvard academic Frances Frei. Much of her thinking can be found online. In addition, *On Purpose* explores how purpose can be used to create distinctive and purposeful experiences that customers love. *Managing the Customer Experience* is probably the seminal work.

In addition to the specific subject areas we have listed here we have also identified a number of books that contain useful perspectives and tools that may be useful for those in engaged in the science and art of brand building. Some are briefly reviewed below. All are included in the list of Further reading at the end of the chapter.

Good to Great
Explores how businesses can become category-leading and world-class.

Aaker on Branding and *Brand Portfolio Strategy*
Explore the 20 principles for building effective brands and developing a portfolio strategy.

How Brands Grow (Parts 1 and 2)
While we may not agree with the all of the content in these books makes for a stimulating read, debunking popular misconceptions and offering a perspective on the impact of digital on brands.

We would also point you in the direction of the *Harvard Business Review* and McKinsey, both of which publish regular research and articles on the subject of brands and branding.

So as we have hopefully demonstrated, there are some definitive tools, some great thinking and a range of effective processes available to support the practitioner but, importantly, none of these should be considered as a replacement for genuine insight and creative thinking. Brands should be built on clear insight; they should be relevant and distinctive and they should excite and empower the customer. Creating them is hard work and involves a melding of IQ and EQ. There are tools to guide the practitioner and to provide shortcuts but they should never replace the human factor that sits at the heart of every successful brand.

Further reading

Brand architecture

Jon Edge and Andy Milligan, *Don't Mess with the Logo*, FT Prentice Hall, 2009
Paul Temporal, *Advanced Brand Management*, Wiley Online, 2010. https://onlinelibrary.wiley.com/doi/book/10.1002/9781119199670

Brand building

David Aaker, *Brand Portfolio Strategy*, Free Press, Simon & Schuster, 2004

David Aaker, *Aaker on Branding*, Morgan James Publishing, 2014

Jim Collins, *Good to Great*, Random House, 2001

Byron Sharp and Jenni Romaniuk, *How Brands Grow*, Parts 1 and 2, Oxford University Press, Part 1 2010, Part 2 2015

Brand experience

Shaun Smith and Andy Milligan, *On Purpose: How to deliver a branded customer experience people love*, Kogan Page, 2015

Shaun Smith and Joe Wheeler, *Managing the Customer Experience*, Pearson Education, 2002

Brand naming

Tom Blackett, *Trade Marks*, Palgrave Macmillan, 1998

John Murphy, *Brand Strategy*, Prentice Hall, 1990

Brand valuation

David Haigh, *Brand Valuation: Managing and leveraging your brand*, Institute of Canadian Advertising, 2000. www.markenlexikon.com/texte/brandfinance_brand_valuation_leverage_may_2000.pdf

Jan Lindemann, *Brand Valuation: The economy of brands*, Palgrave Macmillan, 2009

IN CERTAIN TYPES OF BUSINESS, BRANDS DON'T REALLY MATTER

We have yet to find a sector in which a business didn't need some kind of brand to help it win and retain customers.

Many people seem inherently suspicious of brands and the practice of branding. This may have something to do with the myths we are seeking to debunk here. But it may also be because there is some genuine confusion about what a brand does and how brands operate in different categories. In spite of this cynicism and confusion, we have yet to find a category or industry sector (at least in a functioning market economy) in which a business didn't need some kind of brand to help it win and retain customers.

We are always amused by the story that even in the Soviet Union (where brands were generally not the thing) people began to place a higher value on products manufactured at one plant than another. For example those fortunate enough (or high enough in the state bureaucracy) to be given a car would try and get hold of one made at the plant with the better reputation. The manufacturer's stamp was unwittingly becoming a brand.

Evolution of brand

In a functioning market economy, brands effectively work as short-hand. They started out simply being a guarantee of provenance or quality – at its most basic, a farmer branding his livestock. As the centuries passed and economies grew in size and sophistication, so brands became more complex and more prevalent. The rise of post-war consumerism saw brands act as identifiers, helping consumers to make quick, easy, reliable choices amid an ever-growing litany of choice. By the 1980s we had so much choice and so much emphasis on the individual that brands became a form of self-expression. You could align yourself with specific lifestyle brands and use them to communicate how you wanted to be seen.

By the turn of the millennium, brands were being used to help people escape everyday reality and help them feel special. 'Bling bling' became the colloquial expression for an explicit demonstration of wealth and success. Luxury brands sought to extend their appeal and, as brands like Burberry will attest, some of these decisions finished up causing longer-term problems. Luxury brands over-extended their offers and their greater familiarity and availability actually began to erode their premium positioning. More recently, as people have begun to exercise greater scrutiny over what they buy and they have better understood the power that social media gives them, we have seen brands take on a deeper meaning and significance, connecting with people at a more fundamental level.

How brands work

Yet throughout these much-vaunted 'epochs' two things have remained largely unchanged. In a functioning free market economy, the role of a brand is to generate (or stimulate) demand and help sustain (promote) loyalty. A brand is valuable because it helps to create demand (which can also support a price premium or prevent price erosion) and because it makes it easy for satisfied customers to buy you again (a promise of future satisfaction). Once this is understood, you can start looking at specific categories and better understand how brands work.

There are some categories and sectors that are effectively regarded as commoditized. There is so much availability and so little opportunity to add value to the base product that customers will tend to pay only cursory attention to who provided or manufactured the product. The brand plays a very small role in influencing the purchase decision. Petrol, heating oil, fruit and vegetables might be such categories. But small is not the same as unimportant. In every commoditized category, there will be businesses that have still managed to establish successful brands: think of Texaco, Pink Lady apples, Sainsbury's Organics, Duchy Organics. Each of these brands has managed to build a distinctive profile and as a consequence generate additional demand and sustain loyalty. The New Zealand Kiwifruit Marketing Board has even successfully managed to brand its humble product as Zespri!

How brands support pricing

Within certain categories the importance of a brand on the purchase decision varies according to different price points. Consumer PCs serve as a case in point. Many customers just want a cheap, reliable computer that won't let them down, and customers are wise to the fact that in this sector manufacturers share components and technology and are in many cases assembling machines from what is effectively a global parts bin. In these instances the role of the brand is relatively low; it is sufficient to be a 'known' manufacturer with a reasonable record for fulfilment and reliability. Yet as soon as you start looking at the more premium PCs the role of the brand starts to become disproportionately more important. If we are spending upwards of £2,000 on a piece of equipment, we want to know what makes it different, how reliable it is, how easy it is to upgrade, how customizable it is and what the service support is like. At this point the role of the brand has become more important because we want a product that feels like it justifies its price premium and we want to reduce the risk of it all going wrong. So buying an established and credible brand like Dell or Lenovo starts to make sense.

Brands as key drivers of the purchase decision

Branding works a bit differently in fashion and apparel. Here, the role of brand is typically much more significant than the categories just mentioned. In fashion a large element of where you choose to shop or how much you are willing to pay is largely determined by your perception of the brand. When a customer chooses to shop in Topshop, New Look or Primark they are effectively entering a curated environment. These brands are offering the thrill of fast fashion at extremely competitive prices. These brands are generating huge demand, high volume and a loyal base of customers. Similarly, at the luxury end of clothing and apparel the brand is likely to be *the* primary influence on your decision to purchase. When you buy a piece of luxury clothing or apparel you are buying into a complex and valuable set of tangible and intangible associations. In categories where the role of brand is very high, you will often see brands being deployed in a variety of different ways in order to achieve value for the retailer.

Brands as orchestrators

When you visit an Aldi or a Lidl supermarket (a category where brand is at least moderately important) it might at first feel as though you have entered a kind of anti-brand parallel universe, a place where the joke is on the established consumer goods brands that offer a product reference for own-branded goods and on the people who choose to shop elsewhere. Yet here too branding is being used to generate demand and sustain loyalty. Aldi and Lidl cut their teeth in one of the most competitive retail markets in the world, Germany. Their whole model depends on offering customers reasonable quality at very low prices, which in turn is made possible through offering a no-frills retailing environment and massively restricted choice. Yet largely by virtue of the 'new' and 'novel' brands found inside these supermarkets, most of the customers don't really notice the restricted choice. The own-label brands underpin the value proposition and the novel brands are mostly the smaller, little-known European manufacturers who have been approached by Aldi or Lidl and offered major distribution opportunities in exchange for highly competitive pricing.

Brands continue to endure

A few years ago, many commentators thought that digital would eventually kill off brands altogether. Their point was that our ability to instantly compare products and services would remove the need for any kind of shorthand or broader emotional affinity. If product and price became all that mattered, branding would simply be a signpost. However, the sheer growth and prevalence of digital brands is making that observation look premature. The truth is that people like brands. In fact, they want them. Google, Facebook, Airbnb, Uber, Deliveroo, eBay, PayPal, Compare the Market, ASOS, Farfetch are just a few examples of the thousands of digital brands that accompany our daily lives, catering for everything from the mundane to the super niche. People like to belong to something they feel an affinity with – people who think like them and have similar requirements and expectations.

The perception that many of us now have less time to live our lives, combined with the sheer quantity of daily messaging to which each of us are exposed, may be making us less inclined to think deeply about brands. Digital may be providing us with more opportunities or at least making it easier to be promiscuous but this hardly represents an existential threat. Customers will continue to seek out shorthand for the new, the novel and the reassuring and will still revisit the brands that deliver something appealing or valuable. In 2017 the WPP BrandZ annual league table estimated the cumulative value of the top 100 brands, which is essentially an assessment of their collective ability to generate demand and sustain loyalty, at an eye-watering $3.6 trillion. And those top 100 brands included Amazon, Apple, Facebook, Google, Microsoft, Netflix and YouTube.

Brands matter in any business

There is often more scepticism around the relevance of brands in business-to-business markets. Hard-nosed CFOs operating in highly competitive sectors like manufacturing and technology are often reluctant to invest significant amounts of money in what they see as flimsy intangibles. When presented with such a circumstance it is often helpful to remind those present of the cliché that 'No one ever got fired for hiring IBM'. There in a nutshell is the point. Brands matter in business because ultimately business is personal. Humans like to think they are incredibly rational in their decision-making but there is plenty of relatively new evidence that points to the contrary. The Nobel Prize-winning economist and writer Daniel Kahneman's book *Thinking, Fast and Slow* is an exploration of our cognitive biases. He argues that even when making complex purchase decisions we tend to buy emotionally and then justify rationally. A business purchaser is often looking to gain a competitive advantage, minimize risk and secure a cost-effective and reliable business partner. A brand can be helpful across all of these motivations. It highlights uniqueness, mitigates perceived risk, demonstrates value for money and conveys a sense of stature and reliability.

Boeing, Rolls-Royce and Airbus: all of these businesses invest heavily in their brands. Nothing will ever displace their primary focus on the quality and reliability of their engineering, manufacturing and servicing – and nor should it – but their brand is still important. When products offer similar levels of performance and product excellence then *why* or *how* you do business assumes a greater importance.

Brands in professional services

The same applies for professional services and business consultancy. It is true that when you are buying professional services you will typically place a large amount of importance on the people who will be working on your business. But who they work for is still important. Accenture, Deloitte, EY and PwC all invest considerable amounts of money in their corporate brands. A well-respected brand is usually a prerequisite for any consultancy wishing to be invited to participate in a potentially lucrative pitch. Of course, as a professional services business your brand also helps you attract the talent and develop the thinking and IP required to win business in the first place.

Sometimes people say that it is a company's reputation that influences them. But reputation is effectively a synonym for brand. Both are the particular perceptions and associations that are specific to your company's products or services.

There's value in emotion

People's attachment to brands in any sector should not be under-estimated. How irritated are you when you can't find your favourite coffee shop? How indignant do you become when some-one suggests that you should have bought a different brand? How passionate when someone suggests that you should have bought a new PC as opposed to a £2,500 Mac? What happens when a supplier changes the name or specification of a component or some aspect of their service without publicizing it? Why do we care so much if a product is made of Gore-Tex versus another type of performance fabric?

Across nearly all markets and sectors there are opportunities, however small, to differentiate and add value to the customer. As a consequence brands will continue to remain important driv-ers of enterprise value, helping a product or service to be actively preferred by an increasing quantum of customers as well as encour-aging repeated purchase.

How brands contribute to value

Brands can also help to protect a business from competitive and regulatory threats. A strong brand comprising a unique mix of functional and emotional attributes is difficult for a competitor to meaningfully and legally copy. It is difficult and expensive to sustain true product advantage but easier to protect your intellectual prop-erty and all of the positive associations that are vested within it.

A strong and established brand is also a good guarantee of future earnings. As an investor you can be reasonably confident that in the years ahead Coca-Cola will continue to remain relevant, navigate regulatory requirements and generate solid revenues. The same may not apply to other brands in the sector. It is for this reason that

Apple, Google, Microsoft, Coca-Cola and Amazon are regularly considered by many surveys to be among the world's most valuable brands. It is highly likely that these brands will continue to generate strong revenues and profits in the years ahead.

Brands have a part to play in nearly all aspects of a functioning free market economy. They help to drive value, maintain competitive advantage and are highly protectable. Brands help businesses connect with and retain customers. And customers are the lifeblood of any business.

Further reading

Daniel Kahneman, *Thinking, Fast and Slow*, Penguin, 2012
WPP BrandZ Report: www.wpp.com/wpp/marketing/brandz/
    brandz-2017

BRANDING HAS NOTHING TO DO WITH THE CUSTOMER EXPERIENCE

*Brands need to consistently offer a distinctive,
coherent and memorable customer experience and
they need to accept that their customers will have no
problems sharing both the good and the bad.*

It is true that brands (and by extension branding) are often thought about in terms of identity and attribution *to an owner*. This is understandable: in earlier times brands were used primarily as a means of identification and authentication, delineating both provenance and quality. A visual identity, usually comprising a marque, a graphic system and a photographic style, is a visible asset often widely applied across the customer experience and purposefully designed to be both distinctive and memorable. (Note that 'tangible' means touchable, so is strictly used to refer to those assets you can actually touch – factories, inventory etc.) Ask people in the street in most developed countries to name some well-known brands and it is highly likely that they will reference ones such as Apple, BMW, Coca-Cola, Levi's, Mercedes and Pepsi. It is also highly likely that as they prepare to respond to the question their minds will fill with a heady mix of iconic brand identities and a host of positive or negative associations. Ask most people to draw (from memory) the identities of these brands and it is highly likely that most will be able to make a passable attempt at the apple, the 'propeller', the script, the red label, the star and the circle. Billions have been spent establishing these associations in your mind, so it is not that surprising that when people are asked to think about brands or branding they naturally default straight to the *visual* identity. Yet, in spite of the fact that billions of dollars have been spent building up this valuable instantaneous recognition, it is really just the start of a much bigger story.

A brand is what a brand does

While recognition and attribution are fundamental to the process of brand building, what you actually think and feel about a brand is really the sum of all of the individual experiences you have had with that particular brand. In today's world building successful brands (of any shape or size) is intimately connected to the orchestration of the customer experience. Branding across almost every imaginable sector has everything to do with the customer experience.

Let's start with a powerful illustration of this point. Apple is a highly successful global technology brand that on any given day (stock market permitting) can accurately be described as the most valuable company in the world. This incredible ascendancy has been achieved in a remarkably short amount of time, first under the direction of founder Steve Jobs and more latterly under the aegis of his successor Tim Cook. In the past twenty years, Apple has become one of the most revered brands on the planet and it did so through a single and relentless focus on the quality of the customer experience. Steve Jobs always believed that the way to win in personal computing was to focus on the end-to-end experience. To provide stunningly designed devices that were intuitive, connected and pleasurable to hold and interact with. Jobs believed that computers (and later devices) were there to serve people and that as a consequence they should be simple and easy to use. That observation alone turned out to be visionary, but what really made Apple a global success was the extent to which Jobs ruthlessly implemented this belief across the totality of the customer experience. Jobs' first act upon being reappointed interim CEO of Apple in 1997 was to cull a huge quantity of products and development projects in order to focus the company on the few products he believed would transform the company. Jobs and by extension Apple are the definitive example of the notion that less is more.

The importance of focus and attention to detail

The deeper that you delve into the Apple story the more you see this singularity in evidence. Jobs intuitively understood that devices didn't need to be faceless boxes. He used design to create beautiful elegant minimalist devices that became coveted consumer items. He famously spent as much time designing the insides of his devices as he did the outside. He pushed his people to create powerful, innovative devices that worked seamlessly with proprietary operating systems. He integrated his devices into broader ecosystems, allowing Apple to manage the totality of the user experience while at the same time using technology to accelerate the disruption of entire industries. iTunes, for example, finished up changing the music industry forever. The same care and attention to detail was applied to packaging and what became the ritual of 'unboxing'. He created iconic advertising and completely reinvented high street retailing. Apple stores became experience centres where customers could come and play with the products and resolve technical issues.

The clean and uncluttered stores with hardly any products visible for sale finished up breaking all sales records.

The amazing thing about Apple is that with a few notable exceptions they were using technology and techniques that were available to everyone else, but it just chose to bring them together in a way that surprised and delighted the customer and they did it with a unique level of ruthless intentionality.

Experience matters for all types of brand

Apple serves to illustrate the importance of orchestrating a powerful customer experience, but it also shows just how many aspects of the experience need to be thought about. Granted some brands are in a better position than others to offer immersive and engaging experiences (airlines, restaurants, entertainment centres etc) but that doesn't mean that experience is unimportant for all types of brand. In most service businesses the only way that a unique idea or business model can be brought to life is via the customer experience. Amazon, Dell, Metro Bank and Ikea would all be immeasurably weaker if they hadn't chosen to manifest their purpose through key aspects of their customer experience.

Product brands are also realizing the power afforded by generating memorable experiences. Red Bull, the highly caffeinated soft drink, is a brand literally built upon the idea of memorable and stimulating experiences. It promotes and supports a whole variety of mainstream and niche extreme sports, from F1 through to air racing and even sky diving. Brands like Coca-Cola, Gillette, Heineken, O2 and Visa are using festivals as ways of building direct relationships with customers. They will seek to provide relevant and engaging ways of enhancing the festival-goers experience from virtual catwalks, through to charging centres and even the provision of miniaturized beer tents. Dollar Shave Club demonstrated how new technology can be used to completely reinvent the relationship we have with our razor. In doing so, it has become a brand that has completely disrupted the way we think about an established product category.

The same is also happening in the business-to-business sector.

We like to think that in a business context we buy products and services on a purely rational basis but increasing amounts of new evidence point to the fact that we tend to buy emotionally and justify rationally, regardless of what we are buying. The truth is we value the quality of our interactions in business as much as we do in our personal lives. The big four advisory businesses have collectively invested millions of dollars in improving their customer experience. Manufacturing businesses like Rolls-Royce and GKN have invested billions in updating their systems and processes, allowing them to be efficient real-time partners to their customers. American Express has completely reinvented itself; it is no longer just a payment card but also a whole business expense ecosystem, a data business helping clients to keep control of their expenditure.

Be bad at the things your customers don't care about

Businesses and brands are realizing that customer experience is intimately connected to the art and science of brand building and they are pursuing it with a renewed intentionality. Rather than attempting to make every aspect of their business perfect, the more enlightened brands have realized that in order to create memorable customer experiences they first have to prioritize. As the Harvard academic Francis Frei says: 'In order to be good at something a business generally has to be bad at something else, it just needs to make sure that its customers don't care about the thing it is bad at.' In simple terms Frei is highlighting that it is not economically viable to simply address everything. If you have ever tried to speak to anyone in customer services at Apple, you will know that you generally can't. Apple serves customers on its terms and because of everything else Apple has done well, its customers generally don't seem to mind. Enlightened businesses are realizing that in order to bring their brands to life they must prioritize and adopt a set of distinctive product or service hallmarks. These hallmarks target the important moments of truth in the typical customer experience and are designed to either maximise pleasure or minimize pain.

The value of hallmarks

Virgin Atlantic does this very effectively. Every aspect of the customer experience has been carefully thought about and hallmarks are evident at key points of the experience, most notably at the start, middle and end of your journey. For example, Virgin Atlantic knows that for business customers (travelling in first class) getting to the airport is often a key pain point and so it provides these customers with an integrated app that enables them to check in remotely and monitor the status of their flight and limousines that take them from their destination to designated VIP check-in areas, making progress through the airport as simple and easy as possible. Virgin provides customers with great lounge experiences; inside a Virgin Clubhouse; customers can choose items from a complimentary à la carte menu, visit the games room or spa, or even take a shower before boarding. Once on board and inflight, the same customers benefit from comfortable seats that turn into beds and can enjoy a drink at the cocktail bar. Virgin Atlantic has done everything it can to make the middle part of the flight interesting and memorable – including providing first class customers on overnight flights with their own complimentary pyjamas. Once the aircraft reaches its final destination passengers are also offered the opportunity to take a shower and refresh at their Revival Lounge. Virgin Atlantic understands the fundamental importance of 'fixing it or featuring it'. Virgin knows that it can't do much about its customers having to sit in a pressurized metal tube at 30,000 feet for hours at a time, so it tries to make a virtue of the available time, making it as enjoyable and memorable as possible. Virgin Atlantic understands what matters to its most valuable customers and so it delivers a set of distinctive well-timed hallmarks that seek to differentiate it from the competition.

The rise of the experience economy

Back in 1999 in their book *The Experience Economy,* the economists Joseph Pine and James Gilmour announced that developed economies were about to enter a new economic age. They asserted that just as we had been through the agrarian economy, the industrial economy and the service economy, we were now entering the experience economy. The book was highly influential and while some of its predictions were (with the benefit of hindsight) a little exaggerated, it was nonetheless remarkably prescient. The central tenet of the book is the idea that as we all have increased (or increasing) access to more and more products and services, we will begin to place a higher value on things that offer a distinctive or unique experience, with the highest value of all being placed on those experiences that offer personal transformation. A quick glance at any number of the more popular social media sites would seem to bear this out – a huge proportion of social media activity involves the sharing of personal or collective experiences. We place significant value on what we experience and we have no hesitation celebrating the good and sharing the bad.

Virgin is a brand that intuitively understood the power of transformative experiences. It has built up an impressive portfolio of business interests by choosing to enter markets where customers have traditionally been poorly served. Sometimes on their own and often with other groups of investors, Virgin has helped set new standards in sectors such as airline travel, train travel, financial services, health care and even your local gym. Virgin looks for markets where it can change the game and offer customers a better customer experience. Virgin currently has over 29 different business interests operating under the Virgin brand and while not all of them are trailblazers, many have managed to transform service expectations. Richard Branson is currently working on being the first to offer customers practical and affordable space travel!

Some will no doubt feel that we have already left the experience economy behind and are now entering a fifth age, a new era of enhanced technology and AI. While it is undeniable that technology is accelerating our capability and transforming lives, it appears very much as though technology will continue to be deployed (on the whole) to further enhance and improve the way we experience and interact with the world. Thus the experience economy is still very much in its infancy and technology will be used to serve up more relevant, more engaging and more immersive experiences. In a world of automated processes and artificial intelligence it seems likely that we will place an even higher value on human connections and memorable or unique experiences.

Technology is transforming our expectations

Aside from how technology will be used in the future, it is already radically influencing our current expectations of what good service looks like. Chief among these agents of change is Amazon. This business has revolutionized e-commerce and has fundamentally changed what customers see as a good service experience. When it is possible to get next-day delivery across a massive inventory of products with just a few simple clicks, customers' expectations are changed forever. If Amazon can manage to do all of this quickly and accurately then why can't a much smaller retailer manage the same thing? If Amazon can be price competitive and yet still offer seamless returns and accurate product tracking, why can't others? Of course the fact that Amazon made a big bet on the nature of e-commerce and was ultimately proved right is not always understood; customers don't necessarily care how it was achieved or how difficult it will be for others to catch up. The moment Amazon had developed this capability it quickly became the new norm. This is now the new standard for transactional service, the one by which all other businesses and brands are judged – and interestingly, just like Apple, it came from a profoundly customer-centric founder who believed in a new vision for retail.

Amazon is creating seismic shocks across retail. If Amazon can seemingly deliver any product within just a matter of days, how is it that my local car dealer takes six weeks to receive and fit a replacement part for my vehicle? If I decide I want a new bed or mattress delivered, why am I being asked to wait eight weeks before it will appear at my door? Customers don't live in a vacuum; once they have experienced best in class they quickly expect to experience it everywhere else. Of course it is one thing for a digitally native business to disrupt a market but quite another for an established business to meet disruption head-on and completely reinvent itself, but some have managed it.

Some established brands have embraced the digital opportunity

Mainstream high street retailers like Argos and John Lewis have managed to either partly or wholly re-engineer their businesses to meet the challenges and opportunities of a digitally enabled world. Banks too have worked hard to ensure that they come as close as possible to offering their customers an 'omni-channel' experience. Customers are able to interact with all these businesses in any way they choose, via the store, via a plethora of web-enabled devices, via an app or even over the telephone. These brands will be storing your shopping and browsing history, allowing you to jump seamlessly between devices and serving you with relevant highly targeted content and incentives.

As e-commerce continues its inexorable rise, businesses are being forced to rethink what they do with their physical assets – their shops, their showrooms, their warehouses and their distribution networks. In the past physical assets often conferred a distinct advantage. They drove sales, they were the key to effective distribution and they helped raise barriers to entry. Now the picture is more complex. As more and more transactions occur online and customers are turning up at stores and dealerships already familiar with what's on offer, brand owners are turning more of their stores into experience centres. Instead of simply 'selling' products or services, employees are being repositioned as hosts – representatives, guides and educators.

Many retailers offer a range of curated experiences. Nike's flagship stores are in effect immersive brand centres where you enter a series of mini-worlds. The stores offer limited-edition garments and the opportunity to create personalized apparel and footwear. You can even choose to exercise with your local store. BMW has introduced 'genius bars' in some of its larger dealerships, where you can seek help and advice about any aspect of BMW's product range.

It is also true that experiences have a half-life. Once you are recognized for having a distinctive brand experience, it is important that you are able to maintain the momentum. Brands like Nike constantly review the impact of what they are doing and recognize the insight, energy and creativity required to stay in front of the customer.

The changing nature of the retail experience

One well-known consumer electronics brand decided to stop asking its representatives to 'sell' and instead asked them to 'explain'. The brand owner realized that customers were turning up already equipped with some product understanding. The role of the representative was to build on this knowledge and ensure that the customers were equipped with a full understanding of the complete range of products, enabling the customer and not the representative to make an informed decision on the model that was right for them.

Experiences create powerful connections

Experience is intimately connected to brand perception. Not only do our own experiences powerfully shape our perceptions but we in turn also have a large influence on the perception of others. Social media hugely amplifies this effect. Brands need to consistently offer a distinctive, coherent and memorable customer experience and they need to accept that their customers will have no problems sharing both the good and the bad. Brands need to make it easy for customers to share the good stuff and be agile and effective in response to the things that go wrong; to err is human, but to be contemptuous of your customers is a sin that won't so easily be forgiven.

Although it is easy to think about brands in purely visual terms, their power comes from their ability to occupy a space in our minds. A brand is really the unique mix of emotional and rational associations that form as the consequence of all of our interactions with that brand. As customers have grown more sophisticated and experience more highly valued, so brands have sought to build a more distinctive edge to their experience. Technology is helping to accelerate this change, shifting expectations, disrupting established markets and helping brand owners to build new and more compelling experiences. Getting the customer experience right really matters.

Brands are everything to do with the customer experience.

Further reading

B Joseph Pine II and James H Gilmore, *The Experience Economy*, Harvard Business Review Press, 1999, 2011

BRANDING IS ALL ABOUT THE PRODUCT

A brand is much more than just the product alone.
A brand is a composite of hundreds of activities designed
to form and occupy a space in the customer's mind.

This myth is very fashionable. Not only do you hear people regularly assert that brands are just 'puffery', unnecessary and inconsequential, but they will also cite disruption caused by technology as effectively sounding the death knell for brands. Now that we are able to instantly compare everything online, all that really matters is the product itself.

This is a very big myth.

Brands are about so much more than just a product or service. And if they are about to be made irrelevant by technology, then how is it that seven of the top ten most valuable brands in the world (according to Interbrand) are actually technology brands? It doesn't add up.

A brand is a composite. It is the consequence of hundreds of individual decisions and activities and while a product or service usually sits at the heart of a brand it is far from being the only thing that matters.

Brands confer significant advantages

This example taken from the automotive sector will serve to illustrate the point. If we were to find a selection of equivalent cars from a range of different manufacturers, list their key performance criteria on a basic grid and then remove all references to the individual models and brands, we guarantee it would be virtually impossible to tell the models apart. We also suspect you would feel very uncomfortable using the grid as the sole basis for a purchase decision potentially running into the tens of thousands of pounds. The truth is that in nearly all markets, most of the leading companies will be offering customers performance parity. While the product (or service) is important, its characteristics alone are rarely that instructive when it comes to making a choice. The same applies to the ability to instantly compare features and performance: do you think that this means businesses will be more or less likely to seek parity with each other?

Brands matter because they offer an opportunity to compete on more than just the product or service alone. They are also far more difficult to copy. If a brand has managed to occupy a space in your mind, it is going to be difficult to dislodge and is unlikely to be shifted by a competitor brand attempting to copy the same approach. Brands are an important source of differentiation; they foster vibrancy and originality and help brand owners build positive and valuable associations with their customers.

It is very difficult for any brand to differentiate solely on the basis of how good its product is. Features are generally very easy to copy and even innovative brands usually find that competitors are quick to play catch-up. This doesn't mean that the quality and variation in your product or service are unimportant, it's just that without a patent for a specific ingredient or technical innovation a brand is unlikely to keep its particular product benefit unique for very long. There are exceptions, of course. KFC and Coca-Cola have kept their recipes secret for years. Nothing drives quite like a Porsche and no one delivers as comprehensively and as fast as Amazon. Nonetheless there are thousands of examples of product and service innovations that were quickly and effectively copied. The majority of mid-market cars now all contain very similar features. Technology like ABS or Bluetooth connectivity that was once the preserve of just a few high-spec vehicles are now more or less standard across manufacturers. Voice-activated technology like Apple's Siri has been quickly emulated and arguably surpassed by the technology of other providers like Amazon.

Innovative products and services can provide short and some-times even medium-term competitive advantage, but it is rarely sustainable. Even Intel, who designed and patented its own semi-conductor technology, was only able to stay ahead by utilizing the power of an innovative branding approach, positioning itself as a vital ingredient inside other people's machines.

Great brands help differentiate great products

Great businesses are usually centred on a great product or service, but they are sustained by their brands and the power that they give the brand owners to generate demand and sustain revenues. Let's stay with the automotive sector for a moment. When you choose a car, you do look closely at the performance of the product, includ-ing where it is strong relative to the competition, but it is highly likely that your decision to purchase will also be influenced by the strength of the manufacturer's brand. As you whittle down your choices you will be thinking (consciously or unconsciously) about which of the brands you prefer and this preference will be formed from the summary of all of the different interactions you have had with that brand. All that you have ever known about the manufacturer – the advertising, the design of the cars, the dealer experience, the ratings and reviews, the sponsorships and associations as well as personal recommendation and much more – will all combine to leave an impression in your mind. The strength of that impression will dictate the extent to which you are able to identify with, and hence see yourself in, that particular car. Building a brand is about setting an expectation, delivering consistently against that expectation and then finding ways to reinforce the positive experience such that you can be persuaded to buy again.

Whether a customer is buying toothpaste or a smartphone, the role of the brand may vary (in comparison to other factors) but in both cases the customer is buying into much more than just the functional efficacy of the product. Let's take one brand from each of these categories to make the point.

A tale of two brands

Sensodyne (owned by GSK) is one of the world's leading premium toothpastes, just as the iPhone (manufactured by Apple) is one of the world's leading premium smartphones. Both companies deploy similar techniques to help build their brands. Both start with a high-performing product. Sensodyne has proven efficacy around reducing sensitivity and whitening teeth and has a range of innovative technologies designed to further enhance effectiveness. Similarly, Apple starts with a suite of high-performing devices that arguably lead the way in terms of integrated hardware and software performance. Although at very different price points, brand exerts a high degree of influence on both categories – but for different reasons. We need to trust in our toothpaste and believe that at this price point it will deliver proven efficacy. When spending upwards of £600 for a new smartphone we need to feel that the spend is justified and that we will feel good about carrying the device.

So in both cases the brands are deployed to help address this core requirement. Let's look at how else the brand contributes to the product. Let's start with the advertising and communications. Sensodyne always presents itself as the choice of the professionals; this way it can both justify its premium price and get additional support for its core efficacy. Apple does something similar; it is well known that its products are the choice of the professional creative community and it reinforces this message in its consumer advertising. Apple's ads are vibrant, simple and enigmatic. Turning next to availability and on-shelf presence, both brands closely control their availability and distribution. Sensodyne will take great care to ensure that its products are made available at the dentist's and will exert a high degree of control over how and where the product is sold. Apple is famous for controlling availability and distribution. Apple's products are only available through its outlets and online stores and then through a very limited number of premium resellers. Apple wants to control the whole retail experience because it is here that it can reassert what it is that makes the brand distinctive – no one has a store as unique as Apple's.

Then there is the packaging itself. Sensodyne uses premium cues, including lots of white space and carefully drawn graphics to reinforce the associations with professional dentistry, whitening and the patented technology contained within its products. Apple also does this brilliantly. Apple has realized that with a very high-value item, the experience of unwrapping the product is as important as buying it. By modern standards Apple's packaging is both high quality and a marvel of intuitive cardboard design. None of this is by accident. The packaging is designed to hero the unique premium qualities of the product you have bought and to reinforce the creativity and Zen-like simplicity of the Apple ethos.

In these examples we have touched on just three specific touchpoints, sometimes referred to as 'moments of truth', but there are many, many more. What you have hopefully been able to see is how different elements of the brand combine to support the product and the price premium.

Like products, brands will continue to grow in sophistication

As the understanding of how our minds work continues to increase, so will the sophistication with which brands will seek to influence our perception and opinion. Daniel Kahneman in his influential book *Thinking, Fast and Slow* has helped to transform our understanding of what we know about how people think. Kahneman asserts that all of us have two primary modes of thought. He labels these modes System 1 and System 2. The first mode of thinking is largely to do with the intuitive part of our brain that helps us to quickly estimate people and situations and form connections between things. The second mode of thinking is associated with things like solving complex problems or checking the validity of a logical argument. Kahneman acknowledges that he didn't invent these modes but what is new is the extent to which he believes System 1 influences us. This is important to understand because System 1 thinking likes to use heuristics. Heuristics is a term used in psychology to mean mental shortcuts that help us make decisions faster; once you understand these heuristics you can use them to influence customer behaviour.

Practitioners will use these heuristics to help shape your perception of a brand. A good example of this is called 'anchoring'. It turns out that what a person is prepared to pay for something varies according to whether or not that person is given an anchor point. What may have seemed expensive to you may appear less so if you are given an indication of the last price that was paid for that product or service, or if it can be demonstrated that other people with your requirements paid on average a very similar price. Heuristics can get very sophisticated. As well as things like price perception it can be used to shape areas such as perceived quality or efficacy. There is a reason car manufacturers spend a lot of time getting the sound of the door closing just 'right'. A weighty clunk is used by many customers as a heuristic, a shorthand indication of all-round product quality. Brands are about much more than just a good product or service. Today's practitioner must use all of the tools at their disposal to shape and influence customer perception and behaviour.

What then about technology elevating the importance of the product to such an extent that it ushers in the death of the brand? Well, right now this argument doesn't look very convincing.

Technology is providing new opportunities for brands

It is undoubtedly true that in today's world (more than possibly at any other time) a brand will struggle to survive with a fundamentally flawed product or service. What technology has done is magnify the power of customer opinion exponentially. In the past a brand could probably get away with being poor because a disgruntled customer would struggle to tell more than a few people about their experience before they forgot about it and moved on. Not any more. A disgruntled customer can now share or tweet their negative experience to thousands (and sometimes millions) of people in just a few seconds. This has profound consequences for brands. According to research conducted by Adobe, 72 per cent of millennials research and shop online before going to a store, and (according to *Time*) 74 per cent of US customers identify word of mouth as a key influencer in their purchase decision – positive customer testimonials can also increase sales by as much as 34 per cent. For a business to thrive today it must offer (at the very least) an acceptable level of product or service quality. But like many things this also affords brands a fantastic opportunity. If they are able to better understand customers and make effective or well-timed interventions then they also stand a good chance of being celebrated by customers.

Technology has helped to close the gap between what a brand says and what it actually does (or provides) but if anything it has also given good brands more opportunities to be celebrated by their customers for getting things right.

Technology has also made it easier to compare products and services (as well as swap) between competing brands. While this has undoubtedly made things more uncomfortable for some of the established brands, it has also helped to bring a renewed competitiveness to previously moribund markets. The UK energy market is a case in point. While this market is still dominated by the large energy companies the last few years have seen a plethora of new brands entering it with over sixty different brands now competing for your business. Some of these new entrants are bringing new propositions to the market and they are beginning to get traction. Customers are beginning to understand that it pays to shop around.

Don't confuse transformation with demise

Another phenomenon currently underway appears to be the hollowing out of the mid-market opportunity. It appears that to thrive in today's economy, brands need to be either fast-moving and cheap or innovative and expensive. With brands like Amazon transforming speed and delivery and powerful search tools like Google enabling us to find and review products instantly, customers seem much less inclined to want to spend time wandering the isles of mid-market retailers looking for reliable but ultimately unexciting products. Even outside retail, customers appear to want their everyday brands to be cheap and reliable so that it leaves them with room for more indulgent and transformative experiences. Yet while these changes are interesting, it is both lazy and palpably untrue to use them as evidence that brands are being diminished and all that matters now is the product. While technology is definitely disrupting established business models and, in the process, putting some well-known brands under pressure, it is also helping to give birth to new business models and new brands.

It is true that in today's economy few brands can afford to offer their customers consistently poor products and services. But it should be remembered that products and services are just one (albeit important) component of a brand. A brand is much more than just the product alone. A brand is a composite of hundreds of activities designed to form and occupy a space in the mind of the customer. Technology has not removed the need for a brand, nor has it elevated the product to an exalted status. A brand, much more than any individual product or service, is still the best way of building and protecting long-term competitive advantage.

Further reading

Daniel Kahneman, *Thinking, Fast and Slow*, Allen Lane, 2011

CREATING BRAND NAMES IS EASY

*The process of name development needs to be
carefully managed, with names checked for legal
availability and cultural and linguistic suitability. That
is much harder than it sounds.*

This myth is stubbornly persistent. Creating and registering a brand name is not that easy and rarely completely straightforward. There are lots of reasons for this myth but possibly chief among them is that many people seem to believe that they were born with an innate naming ability. In our experience this is rarely the case. Naming seems to be regarded even by many practitioners as essentially an easy undertaking; it just needs a few creatively minded people to get together, drink some coffee and kick around some ideas.

Perhaps if you are a very small business with little ambition and no real understanding of the value of trademarks this is sufficient. In nearly all other cases it is not. If you are a larger business with designs on expansion and you intend to trade internationally then naming is a process that you would be well advised to take more seriously.

Decide if a new name really is required

Before embarking on the creation of a new name, we would always advise that you take the time to determine if a new brand name really is required. It is easy to assume that you need to develop a new brand name when actually all that may be required is a simple descriptor. The job of the practitioner is to keep the proliferation of unnecessary brands to an absolute minimum. Additionally, even before you start creating new names it is always a good idea to look at what you have that could sensibly be repurposed or repositioned. Always look back at your full suite of trademarks; established brand owners often have a large catalogue of largely forgotten names that may possibly be reused.

Brand names can become valuable trademarks

Let's start with the legal and financial implications. Brand names can be registered as trademarks and as such are capable of being legally owned and protected. This is important. Brands can be enormously valuable and while a brand may occupy a space in the mind of the customer the things that help to identify a brand (the marque, the design, the pack shape and even a sound) can most definitely be registered and protected. It is the ability to legally own and protect these tangible assets that crystalliszes the value of a brand.

From a legal and financial perspective, therefore, the most significant aspects of a brand are its trademarks, namely the name and the identity. Any practitioner who wishes to lay claim to more than just a registered domain name needs to be able to register and protect their brand; in effect they need to ensure that their proposed brand name and identity are effectively unencumbered – in other words that something identical or highly similar has not already been developed and is either registered or has a registration pending. This is further complicated by the need to register your name in all of the territories in which you intend to trade and in all of the trademark classes in which you plan to trade. When an informed practitioner wants to get it right from the outset, there are a lot of factors that need to be considered.

The good news is that with a dollop of pragmatism and the support of a decent trademark lawyer many of these complexities can be successfully navigated. Many practitioners will actually be seeking registration in just a few territories and trademark classes and this helps to simplify the process enormously. The EU actually runs a centralized trademark register, making initial checks relatively speedy and inexpensive. A lot of pure-play digital brands will be less inclined to worry about extensive registration across multiple trademark classes.

It is also true that the sheer volume of applications and registrations will mean that you are virtually certain to meet an objection to your registration. In order to be granted a successful registration it is likely that you will be required to compromise and accept a restriction to a specific or more narrow band of trademark classes. You may even find yourself having to negotiate with a third party so that rights in an existing name can be transferred legally to you.

It should be noted that actions are sometimes also pursued for what is known as 'passing off'. This is usually in instances where one brand name is emulating another to such an extent that a customer stands to be genuinely confused and the originating brand financially disadvantaged. Instances like these are typically found in consumer goods markets. While the name and identity are not exactly the same, taken as a whole they are deemed sufficiently confusing for the originating brand to be negatively impacted.

To some extent, the level of complexity associated with the registration process will be dictated by the potential size and scope of the brand. If you are a multinational corporation seeking to launch or rename a billion-dollar brand you are likely to take all of the above factors into account. Nonetheless, big or small, the practitioner is well advised to consider the legal aspects of the naming process before embarking on the journey and incurring time and expense.

What's in a name?

The second part of the process that makes brand naming more complicated is the role of the name in helping to establish or build the brand itself. It is not always apparent to the casual observer, but different types of name can help brand owners achieve different things. Naming is not quite a science but it can be approached more strategically than most people realize.

Just before we explore this area, let's also remember that a brand name – in and of itself – is not the same thing as a brand. A brand is a composite, a mix of functional and emotional attributes that reside in the mind of the customer. To illustrate this point, there are lots of businesses with names that, once seen out of context (and in isolation), seem odd or even possibly unsuitable. Starting from scratch would you have chosen *Boots* for the name of a chemist? Would you have chosen *Dunhill* (one letter different from 'dung hill') for a name to adorn a range of upmarket gentlemen's products? When you go to a computer store and ask for an *Apple*, do you expect to be given a small, green fruit? We suspect not. The point is that applied in a brand context these words have largely lost their original associations and now stand for completely different sets of meanings and associations. A brand name is an important identifier but recognizing its inherent role and flexibility is key to making the most of the naming opportunity.

The descriptive name

There are essentially three categories of brand name, each with pros and cons, and these names are probably best thought of as occupying a particular position across a broader spectrum. At one end of this spectrum we have descriptive names. These are names that are either wholly or broadly descriptive of what it is that the brand actually does. *Compare The Market* is a fine example of a descriptive

Figure 5 The naming spectrum

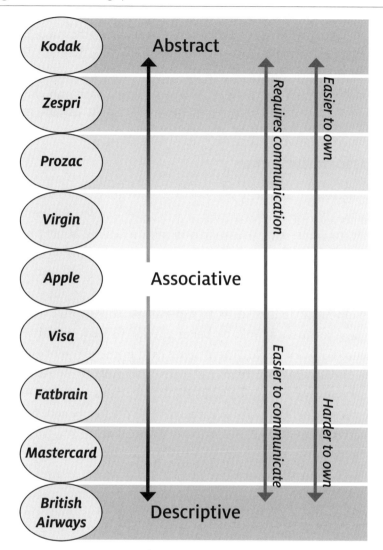

name; customers are not going to be left in any doubt about what it is that this brand does. Similarly *British Airways* is a straightforward description of what the brand does, as is *Pizza Hut* or digital behemoth *Facebook*. As well as telling you what a brand is or does, a descriptive name can also describe a combined action or feeling, for example *PayPal*. Descriptive names are helpful because they need very little explanation or qualification. They can be efficient at launch and are much in evidence across the digital space. Nonetheless by virtue of their descriptive nature they can be much more difficult to successfully register and protect. As a general rule of thumb, the more descriptive a word is the more difficult it is to legally register it.

The associative name

The situation is different for the next category of name on the spectrum, the associative name. Associative names are generally designed to create a clear association with a desired benefit or feeling and have the advantage of being less descriptive and so generally easier to register. The drawback is that associative names lose the benefit of being immediately understandable and so may require more support or qualification. In some cases a descriptive word can be made associative simply by being applied in a completely different context. For example, *Apple* being used in the realm of personal devices and computing. *Twitter* is a great example of an associative name; it conveys a sense of what the service does and how it feels to use the service. *LinkedIn* is associative of the key benefit of using their networking service. *Google* is a misspelling of *googol*, which is the name of a large number (10^{100}) and designed to associate the service with the enormous power of its search engine. *Virgin* is associated with doing something for the first time and is used to reinforce the sense that Virgin always looks at a market opportunity from a fresh perspective and deliberately tries to challenge the status quo. Associative names can be used to disrupt conventions in a market. When Hutchison Whampoa launched its brand *Orange* into the UK mobile telephony network market, it was so different as a name from names like *Cellnet* and *Vodafone* that it created enormous interest. Associative names are often used in prescription drugs where in theory manufacturers are prohibited from communicating efficacy or specific benefits. *Viagra* and *Prozac* are classic examples of names designed to create if not definitive benefits then certainly positive associations.

The abstract name

The final category of name is abstract names. These names are either entirely made up or else comprise acronyms or the melding of names and syllables. Famous examples of abstract names include *Kodak* and *Xerox*. Few people can remember that *IBM* was once International Business Machines. *McDonald's* is just a surname that has come to mean something over time. *Tesco* was created when Jack Cohen bought a shipment of tea from Thomas Edward Stockwell. He made new labels using Stockwell's initials (TES) and the first two letters of his own surname (Co). Abstract names are often used for corporate holding companies or when very large companies are rebranded, the drinks group *Diageo* being a good example. Abstract names are by definition generally easier to create and register but have the disadvantage of requiring lots of help and support to get them established.

By now it will hopefully be evident that brand naming should be approached carefully and thoughtfully. Time spent considering these factors will make the development of your naming brief much more effective.

Naming is emotional

The third reason why brand naming can be difficult is that it can often become highly emotional. Brand owners and customers can become powerfully attached to brands and this can make the process of renaming highly emotive, especially in instances where brand owners are concerned. As the brand name often becomes synonymous with the brand itself, huge significance is therefore placed on getting the name 'right' but with very little understanding of how the quest for a suitable name can be directed. The litany of high-profile naming failures also does little to calm the nerves of uncertain business leaders. Many are haunted by the public criticism they remember for names like *Consignia* or *Monday* (new names for the Royal Mail holding company and a PwC spin-off consultancy respectively; neither name lasted). Few appreciate that a clear naming brief can help avoid many of the naming pitfalls. Yes, the process of creating a great brand name still requires skill and creativity but the chances of success are increased with a clear process and a tight set of evaluation criteria

Naming can require linguistic and cultural understanding

The fourth and final reason why creating a brand name is often more difficult than people realize is that developing a name is a creative process often being undertaken in a broader cultural context. A small business looking to trade within a single country has arguably an easier time than a much larger business looking for a name that can be used globally. Not only does a name have to be capable of being registered it also needs to be able to work effectively across diverse cultures. This doesn't necessarily mean that a name has to be fully understood in all regions of the world (it can still act as an effective identifier) but ideally it will avoid any negative cultural or linguistic connotations. There have been many famous examples of this going wrong and perhaps one of the most famous examples was the launch of GM's car the *Nova*. It turned out that in Spanish *no va* means 'It doesn't go', which perhaps didn't help sales of the car in Spanish-speaking countries, especially in South America. An automotive name that fared much better was the Ford *Mondeo* a name derived from the Latin for 'world', a much better connotation for Ford's first genuinely global car.

Not only do global names need to translate well but they need to be sensitive to transliteration too. A name might sound perfectly fine in one culture but sound incredibly rude in another. Brands need to think carefully about how their names will be received in different cultures. *Nora Knackers* is a good name for a crispbread brand if you are in Norway, less so in the UK. Rolls-Royce thought *Silver Mist* had premium associations to the British customer, but 'Mist' is a very different four-letter word to a German customer! Western brands in places like the Middle East or Asia will often run dual versions of their names and in China they are often given a completely different name to the one the owner may have intended. Of course in the end the brand name will be accompanied by the brand identity (especially important where literacy rates are low) and the idea is to create a clear set of identifiers, ones that clearly distinguish your brand in the eyes of the customer.

This gives brand names that are based on a surname or set of initials a distinct advantage. It is perhaps not that surprising that many of the world's most successful brands have names that derive from individuals or acronyms. *IBM, GE, McDonald's, BMW, Disney, Louis Vuitton, Honda, SAP, H&M, Zara, UPS, JP Morgan*: all appear in the top 30 of Interbrand's Best Global Brands 2017. Anyone embarking on the creation of a global brand name would do well to ensure that those charged with developing the names are either good linguists or people with access to a relevant network of people who can give feedback on the relevance and suitability of any proposed name.

The advantages of a clear process

The best naming processes are the ones that start with the understanding that the journey is unlikely to be simple and straightforward. Practitioners need to bring a mix of legal, strategic, creative and commercial skills to the table. Take the time to develop a long list of names for identical checks, accept that you will lose some of your favourites along the way, check your preferred names against your strategy and recognize that even your chosen name is unlikely to be entirely problem-free. Commercial pragmatism and an understanding that nothing is entirely free of risk are an important part of getting a good result.

Creating a brand name can look easy and sometimes it can be. The small trader or domestic entrepreneur is unlikely to get too vexed by the process and will probably worry about trademark registration much later on. For most other businesses, though, the process of name development needs to be approached more carefully. There is much to be gained by understanding whether a new name is required and then, if it is, where it will appear and how it will be used. Once the practitioner is clear about this, they can identify the category of name that they think will be most helpful and write a clear naming brief. The process will then need to be carefully managed, with prospective names being checked for both legal availability and cultural and linguistic suitability – get this right and it will be possible to spend time creating interesting and protectable names.

Proceed with caution. There's more to a name than is at first apparent.

Further reading

Best Global Brands 2017: http://interbrand.com/best-brands/
    best-global-brands/2017/ranking

BRANDS ARE JUST CONSUMER GOODS

*A brand is what your name represents in the mind of
your customer, your employee and anyone else whose
opinion about you counts. And that is true whatever
you sell.*

In 1996 Interbrand published a book called *The World's Greatest
Brands*. Top of its list of 100 names was McDonald's. It seems extraordinary now but at the time this caused controversy. The controversy
was not just about whether McDonald's was really a greater brand
in the world than Coca-Cola, which for many people was the obvious epitome of a global brand and which had longer heritage and
greater distribution than the Golden Arches. The controversy was
also because some people did not think McDonald's was a brand
at all. In fact, some market researchers told us that McDonald's
couldn't be a brand because it wasn't a product. Actually, that was
not as daft then as it sounds now. At the time, the popular conception of brands among the marketing and business community was
that brands were packaged goods.

A brand was a product on the shelf – nothing else

Unless you literally went into a shop and could choose clearly and physically between two competing branded products in the same category side by side on a shelf, with the same or similar price point, you could not be making a brand choice. You may be making choices based on other attributes associated with the brand name – the fact that you want a particular type of hamburger, the fact that it's in a convenient carry-away package in a conveniently located store, or that it serves good-value food for the family. But these were not considered brand drivers. They were drivers of customer choice but not, it seemed, drivers of brand differentiation. It was the same for anything that wasn't designed, manufactured or produced. Banks, airlines, supermarkets. They were all companies. McDonald's was a company. And companies had corporate identities, whereas products had brand identities.

The Top 10 Global Brands identified by Interbrand in 1996 were:

1 McDonald's

2 Coca-Cola

3 Disney

4 Kodak

5 Sony

6 Gillette

7 Mercedes-Benz

8 Levi's

9 Microsoft

10 Marlboro

Compare that to their list in 2016:

---

1   Apple (*18th in 1996*)

2   Google (*didn't exist in 1996*)

3   Coca-Cola (*showing the enduring strength of a well-managed brand*)

4   Microsoft (*up 5 places in 20 years*)

5   Toyota (*up from 31st*)

6   IBM (*11th*)

7   Samsung (*joint 96th with Gordon's Gin in 1996*)

8   Amazon (*just opened its doors in 1996*)

9   Mercedes-Benz (*down just 2 places in 20 years*)

10 GE (*which didn't even place in 1996 because it owned so many independent brands that the folks at Interbrand couldn't work out how to assign a value to it as a corporate brand*)

Furthermore, and for many years, the law had seemed to discriminate in a similar way. Trademarks were applied to products and goods. Retail names like McDonald's were given 'service mark' status in the USA. And even this came about a long time after trademarks were first legally conceived.

Retailers also distinguished between their 'corporate name' and their branded products. Some created standalone brand names to apply to their own sourced products, for example M&S created the St Michael brand to apply to a range of goods (from food to clothes) that were only sold in their shops, partly to address this perception problem of 'goods' being very different from the service of the store in which they were sold. Or they called the products they sourced directly and put their name on as 'own label'. Again, this implied that there were 'branded' goods made by brand owners and 'non-branded' goods supplied by retailers.

These own-label products were typically cheaper and considered of perceivable lower quality. Actually they were often made or sourced from the same factories that were either owned by or supplying the brand owner. *The Sun* reported in 2017 that Weetabix's brand of breakfast cereal actually competes in supermarkets alongside the retailers' own-label wheat biscuits which were also produced by the Weetabix company. It also revealed that other household brands such as McVitie's, Müller, Patak's and Andrex also produce unbranded items for supermarkets.

These manufacturer brand owners might be able to do this because they often have spare capacity on their increasingly efficient production lines.

The supermarket own brand battles

Then, in the mid-1990s, the brand versus retailer own-label wars took off. And suddenly the power of the retailer brand was seen and understood.

The battle started in the UK (and was seen elsewhere) when retailers like Tesco and Sainsbury's began to closely mimic on their own-label packaging the design and graphic cues of leading FMCG brands. Sainsbury's began producing its own label of premium coffee called Gold, with Gold packaging and a label with pictures of coffee beans, all of which looked very similar to Nestlé's Nescafe Gold Blend premium instant coffee. And Sainsbury's sold theirs in a similar-shaped jar. The big difference was in the price, of course. The retailers could sell their similar-looking product at a much lower price than the leading brand. A huge row erupted between the brand owners and the retailers, which became even more complicated when Virgin entered the cola market with a product (produced by Coty) that was in a red can with Virgin Cola in white lettering. Coca-Cola objected. The brand versus own-label brands battle was already complicated enough because of the interdependency of the two protagonists. Nestlé needed the retailers to stock and sell their products, the retailers needed Nestlé both for the sales that brands such as Nescafé generated but also because those brands set the benchmark against which they could closely develop their own labels.

Eventually a settlement was reached. Nestlé produced more distinctively shaped packaging for their products. The shape of the glass jar, for example, was changed to one uniquely designed for them and so more legally protectable. Sainsbury's and other retailers who could neither afford to invest in highly customized packaging formats nor wanted to continue to fight their vital suppliers agreed to ensure they would respect the intellectual property rights of the brand owners.

Two enduring legacies emerged from this battle. One was the British Brands Group, originally established to help lobby for legislation to protect against rip-offs, as they interpreted the retailer's actions. Now it lobbies for a wider understanding of the importance and contribution made to the British economy by brands. The other and even more important legacy was a real focus on innovation and differentiation from both sides. This has continued to this day in order to differentiate and distinguish the relative value of offers to consumers.

What the brand versus own-label battle highlighted was the shift in perceptions of who or what was actually a brand. Brands were still consumed as products but in consumers' minds it was now clear that they were associated with a set of trusted values, which could be transferred from one area to another. In the case of Sainsbury's, the credibility of its brand as a grocery retailer enabled it to sell its own-branded groceries. For Virgin, its values of fun and taking on the big guys that were built through its record stores and airlines could be applied – with admittedly limited success – to the category of soft drinks.

In fact, Sainsbury's, Tesco and the like went even further. They realized that what their brands stood for was not a specific type of business called 'supermarketing' but abstract and greatly appreciated values of convenience, price competitiveness, quality and service. This gave them the authority to challenge other markets where incumbent brand owners were vulnerable. Tesco went into financial services and both Tesco and Sainsbury's, among others, began selling their own-branded petrol on the forecourts of their largest superstores and later as dedicated petrol stations to which were attached mini-shops carrying their brand, such as Tesco Express.

So by the mid-1990s, a major shift in the understanding of brands and branding was happening and our researcher friends would soon have to reassess their opinion that McDonald's was not a brand.

Anything could be a brand

It wasn't just retailers who had by now learnt to regard themselves as brands and to operate with the same kind of disciplined processes and thinking as traditional FMCG brand owners. All kinds of other categories got the brand bug.

Banks began to redefine themselves and to rebrand themselves. Moving away from a product or marketing orientation, creating sub-divisions or new financial services with distinct names, they began to focus more attention on the 'corporate' brand and attempted to simplify everything under a single promise or proposition. Barclays redesigned its famous eagle, upgraded and renovated its branches, replaced existing account names and re-badged some of its subsidiary businesses under a global brand identity. HSBC did the same thing on an even bigger scale. Remember the bank brand Midland? It called itself The Listening Bank and used advertising featuring a kindly animated griffin voiced by the popular actor Richard Briers. Well, that all went and became HSBC. To this day, you will find high-profile advertising for HSBC in places such as airports associating it with emotional and aspirational values (like any traditional consumer brand has for years) and positioning it as the world's local bank.

Airlines similarly overhauled their entire portfolio of subsidiary companies. BA branded everything they could with a new 'speedmark' and redesigned BA logo. They ran into a little brand turbulence after a rebrand launch in 1997 when they repositioned themselves as a 'Citizen of the World' instead of as a national airline carrier. To express this positioning, they boldly used a diverse set of multicultural artworks on their tailfins to reflect the routes they flew. It caused a great deal of controversy and famously the then Prime Minister Margaret Thatcher put a handkerchief over a small model plane bearing one of the designs. Eventually, BA adopted one single design based on the Union flag for all its tailfins, things settled down and the global BA branding has been consistent for the past twenty years.

Technology and telecommunications were also becoming branded. When Apple launched its iconic 1984 advert at the Superbowl event of that year, it heralded a complete change in what kinds of things people would see as consumer brands. Computers until then had largely been the preserve of big businesses, governments or educational institutions. In 1977, the CEO of DEC (one of America's largest computer businesses) had confidently asserted that there would be no need for anyone to have a home computer. In the same year, Steve Jobs confidently predicted that his company would help put a computer in everyone's home all round the world. Once the cost of computer hardware and software began to fall and the design and user interface was made more human, suddenly people could not only afford to buy their own personal computer, they positively demanded one. A growing consumer market developed and, like any consumer-driven market, it had competition – and where there is competition, there are brands competing for our attention.

As we know, Steve Job's greatest genius was that he realized not what computers were for but what computing could do. In a speech he gave in 1983 to a small room of listeners in California, he talked about a future in which people would walk around listening to music on tiny computers, watching TV shows, communicating with other people. He saw computing as a means to liberate, educate and entertain people. He saw design-led thinking – graphic, product, software and service design all developed from the point of the experience that the human end-user would most appreciate – as a profound part of Apple's brand DNA. By relentlessly following design-led, consumer-led, brand-led principles, he created a focused range of innovative products and services that have transformed not only what we do but what we mean when we say 'brand'.

Utilities and telecommunications likewise became brand conscious. After decades of mostly state-owned control and consequently monopolistic practices, a tidal wave of deregulation, privatization, free and open market trading turned sectors like electricity, gas, water, and telecommunications into competitive ones. The privatized companies rebranded to shed their old state-owned image. New entrants with shiny new brand names like Orange and then EE, Octopus and Buzz have poured into these markets as they have developed and grown. Virgin brings you your broadband, home and mobile phone services, even if it is no longer selling you cola. People were making brand choices not just by choosing between one comparable set of convenient services and price tariffs but by selecting based on what they 'thought and felt' about the competing branded offers.

You could even have brands within brands, as Intel Inside and NutraSweet showed.

Brands were built even where there were no consumers

Business-to-business brands were also developing. In the early 1990s Louis Gerstner took over IBM and quickly identified that it was too diversified, had business units which did not create enough value and some which made no strategic sense when looked at from the point of view of what IBM stood for. One of the tools he used to help him streamline the global business was brand valuation. It helped him to identify which parts of the IBM empire added value to the brand and which didn't. Of course, behind that was his appreciation of what IBM meant – what the brand represented. IBM's purpose has long been to develop information technologies that help mankind. In its pursuit for smarter ideas for a smarter planet, it has constantly evolved its offer. Thomas Watson, its legendary chairman who coined that purpose back in 1915, would not recognize the types of things the business does now, but he would surely recognize what IBM stood for.

Business-to-business brands abound. Walk through airports or railway stations, leaf through magazines or newspapers and you will see advertising for companies such as SAP or Accenture. The average consumer will never commission Accenture to implement an IT strategy for their house, so why do these companies advertise so publicly? It's brand building. They want their customers, CEOs, CFOs and CTOs to be constantly reminded of their strength, reliability and scale.

Brands became important even in sectors that made no money. Charities began to understand that they were in a highly competitive market – in fact one of the most competitive there is, that of the human conscience. They had to fight for awareness and emotional relevance to ensure that people were prepared to give them the money they needed for their good works. Oxfam underwent a major rebranding exercise globally, bringing all its various subsidiary and affiliated organizations in different countries (which often had different names and logos) under a single Oxfam name and a new highly distinctive logo that could be recognized anywhere in the world as a symbol even where the Roman alphabet letters of Oxfam were incomprehensible.

WWF similarly focused on a global brand with imaginative global campaigns such as its annual Earth Hour where all round the word, people are encouraged to turn off their electricity for an hour to dramatize the amount of energy we are consuming and the consequent pressure we are putting on our planet's resources.

Sports federations such as FIFA rebranded. The World Cup became the FIFA World Cup and a stylized version of the FIFA World Cup trophy (one of the most recognized trophies in the world) became incorporated into every logo every four years. Broadcasters such as CNN, Sky and the BBC turned attention on to their brands as the battle between terrestrial and satellite television morphed into a battle on a digital ground.

Some brands don't make anything at all

The digital world has produced brands that do not make anything at all. Not even their own programmes. Facebook and YouTube essentially curate (at best) but mostly just host content produced by people like you and me or source content that is of interest to you and me. But these are brands nonetheless.

What all of these brands, in whichever category you care mention, understood was that they needed to reflect a personality for their brand; a sense of identity over and above the principal function of their operations or the legal requirement of a trademark. A brand personality, whether serious and reassuring like an IBM or engaging and fun like Facebook, is key to brand preference.

As brand personality became central to the perceived value of a brand, it would only be a matter of time before a personality became a brand.

The rise of the person as a brand

Famous personalities had long been used to confer their particular charisma or credibility on a brand. John Wayne used to endorse

Chesterfield cigarettes many years before his death from lung cancer. Paul Newman developed his own brand of salad sauces. Pop stars and sports stars from George Best to O J Simpson have endorsed their own range of products.

In 1993, the pop star Prince used branding to make a dramatic public and professional statement. He rebranded himself. He dropped the name Prince and instead adopted a graphic device without letters, ♀, the 'Love Symbol'. His decision to rebrand was in response to a long-running contract dispute with his label Warner Brothers and also to his belief that he was being commercially and creatively constrained. In frustration with this, he had written the word 'SLAVE' on his face. By rejecting the brand name Prince, he not only freed himself from metaphorical chains, he had also freed himself from contractual and commercial constraints. His contract with Warner Brothers was with Prince. ♀ was not contracted to anyone.

It was a clever use of the tools of modern commercial marketing against modern commercial marketers.

But all of this was just a warm-up for the big breakthrough in the modern phenomenon of personality as a brand.

In 1996, the same year that Interbrand asserted that McDonald's was not only a brand but the world's greatest one, a future and unique global brand first caught the public eye.

In an English Premier League football match between Wimbledon and Manchester United, a relatively little-known Manchester United midfielder scored an extraordinary goal from within his own half of the pitch. It was an astonishing act of style and skill. Captured by TV cameras, the goal was shown countless times around the world. It was the moment that launched Brand Beckham.

'I couldn't have known it then, but that moment was the start of it all: the attention, the press coverage, the fame,' David Beckham wrote in his autobiography, *My Side*. 'When my foot struck that ball, it kicked open the door to the rest of my life.'

The Beckham brand phenomenon

David Beckham has achieved incredible success on and off the pitch. He once topped a list of the 50 wealthiest players in the world, according to an index that looked at net worth taking salary, endorsements and assets along with outside business interests into consideration. He was closely followed by Lionel Messi, Cristiano Ronaldo and Zlatan Ibrahimovic. Those wealthiest players, according to Goal.com, had a combined wealth of over £1.7bn, which was greater than the GDP of Liberia. Goal.com estimates that Beckham's net wealth is now $400m.

Beckham has become a byword for a new type of brand in the 21st century – an authentic personality brand who can sell different types of products to anyone, anywhere in the world because of what he does and who he is. He is not a single product brand with a manufactured appeal that is communicated relentlessly to the same target audience globally.

The book *Brand It Like Beckham* shows how the Beckham brand has been developed by effectively following the best practices and principles of any great international brand: a clear set of values and image, proper trademark protection, long-term planning, thoughtful communications and extensions. Adidas and other brands would choose celebrities to endorse their products that matched the values of their brand and the desired self-image of their consumers. The Beckhams – because it is not just about David, it is also about Victoria and it might even be about any or all of their children – have done the same thing in reverse. They have been very clear about what they want to stand for and then chosen commercial partners who reflect their values and image.

There are specific reasons why the brand has been so successful.

1 His dedication to football

Football is the world's biggest sport, and it shows no signs of decline. From Seattle to Shanghai, people consume football avidly, on TV, online, on mobile, in the stadium, in the pub, in the papers, in stores and in betting shops. If Beckham were a basketball player, blessed with a similar talent and charm, it is unlikely that he would be this big worldwide.

His enduring dedication to playing football at the highest level appealed to people. Twenty-one years after he made his debut for Manchester United, he was playing at Paris St Germain, in the UEFA Champions League. Beckham is unique in having played for top teams in four of the five main European leagues, with arguably the biggest clubs in each, and he has won every senior club honour of note. And that list of achievement does not even include the US adventure where he helped to raise the profile of the sport.

He was 37 and still playing at the highest level when he topped that Rich List. You cannot fake that level of dedication and longevity. People recognize it and the vast majority admire it. The best brands are based on some genuine product quality and that is true of Beckham's love of football. It's been extended by his decision – foresightedly written into his contract with LA Galaxy back in 2007 – to develop an MLS Franchise in Miami.

2 The appeal of his personality beyond football

He is perhaps the only footballer who could claim to be a household name anywhere in the world, even in houses where no one likes football. He is good-looking and has natural design sensibility, which make him incredibly photogenic in an age that is more visual in its media consumption than ever before and which is obsessed with style, glamour and celebrity.

At the same time, paradoxically for someone so famous, he is humble or down to earth – his manner of speaking is quiet, he is respectful of others, he likes simple pleasures like 'pie and mash' (a dish popular in East London, where he was born) and he has never seemed to lose a sense of his roots. This is important for people who like to see authenticity and not arrogance in their heroes.

Outside football, the Beckham brand is enhanced by his wife's own career. The brand comprises both Victoria and David. Victoria, already a pop star with the Spice Girls (another brand), has had a successful second career with her fashion range. The two of them present a complementary 'his and hers' offer in products such as perfumes. This helps to give near ubiquity to the Beckham name, which helps to keep the brand top of mind.

The way that the Beckham brand has extended beyond David's football career is a great example to any brand manager looking to extend a brand. The Beckham brand is 'consumed' in one way or another by almost every conceivable demographic (age, ethnicity, socioeconomic or sexual definition – almost everyone seems to like Beckham).

3 Their professionalism in managing their business

David and Victoria Beckham own a complex series of legal rights to their names and images, which are properly protected and can be commercially exploited. These rights are intellectual property such as trademarks, copyrights, image rights etc. They are managed via a company – or in their case a series of companies – for different purposes. Huge international companies (Adidas, Armani etc) want to use their image for endorsement, sponsorships, licences and so on, in sectors as diverse as clothing and food supplements. It's a highly complex legal situation, with different legal rights applying in different countries internationally. It needs professional management.

Then there are the products and services and other projects which the Beckhams directly create, own and manage, for example Victoria's fashion range and the Beckham fragrance range.

A unique aspect to the Beckhams is how astute they have been in taking good advice to protect and grow their branded business. They have assembled a strong team around them who clearly under-stand the complex business and legal issues around image rights, commercial ventures and brand building internationally, so that their dealings are profitable and appropriately protect their image.

Their reputation as well as their consumers' rights are protected, preventing people from selling products with Beckham's name or image when they have not been given permission to do so.

An example of this astuteness was the appointment of 19 (XIX) to be their partner in developing the Beckham brand beyond their core product of football and popular music. Simon Fuller, who founded 19, knew Victoria from her days in the Spice Girls so he was someone that they could both trust on a personal and a professional level.

Dealing with the issues to which we have referred above (image rights, the range of activities that they are involved in) as well as the 24/7 media goldfish bowl they live in, requires skills and experience which the average football agent simply would not have. The world is fascinated with the Beckham phenomenon, and global media never switches off. It would be impossible to cope with this level of attention without some highly experienced help. It is also easy to forget that the Beckhams are people with four kids, friends and other family. Maintaining some semblance of normality in the highly exposed world in which they live requires professional help.

You need a good team around you to do that. That means you need to be able to judge, appoint and take the advice of a good team. And the smartest thing that smart people do is know how to take smart advice.

4 His understanding of the 'right thing to do'

Beckham has repeatedly shown the ability to make forward-thinking choices that build a consistent but always engaging story that captures people's imagination. A crucial part of that story is his – and his wife's – desire to give something back to the world. He has gone beyond donations to charity, even beyond setting up foundations. He has become an ambassador for causes and issues that he is concerned about and which are congruent with people's perceptions of him.

Sport and children are enormously important to him, so it's no surprise that he was not only involved in helping to win the bid for London to host the Olympics but played a high-profile role at the opening ceremony too. When he joined Paris St Germain, conscious of the severe economic difficulties that France and the whole of the Eurozone faced, he waived all his revenues from his image rights and donated his estimated €3.5m salary to charity. For five months of that year, he did not earn anything from playing football for the first time since he signed as an apprentice for Manchester United. It was an extraordinary act which earned him praise from many people. We are too often encouraged to be cynical about the motivations of anyone in the public eye. We are especially conditioned to be conscious of marketing spin and PR. However, people see David Beckham as a decent guy who likes to put something back.

Here is an anecdote to support that point. I (Andy) was waiting to go on TV in the UK recently to talk about Beckham. I had to have make-up put on, as most guests do, to stop the glare of studio lights reflecting off their skin on camera. The make-up lady who was looking after me was probably in her late fifties, maybe early sixties. She asked me what I was going to talk about on the show and I said David Beckham. She said: 'Oh, I like him. He's good at what he does and he does good things.' Her words are as good a summary of why Beckham is so popular as a brand as you can get.

Beckham does what a lot of brands wish they could do and which the best ones do: he stays true to his promise, extends his offer appropriately, makes sensible investments, engages with his fan base and stays profitable.

As we said in Chapter 6, brands have economic value not only in the sense that they create value for themselves but also in benefiting a wider economy. The Beckonomics of the brand are that it:

- makes money directly from salaries, bonuses, image rights, sponsorships, licence fees, image rights, merchandise sales, ticket sales
- makes money directly for clubs, sponsors, official commercial partners, agents, employees, entertainment businesses

Figure 6 Goldenballs: How Brand Beckham created value

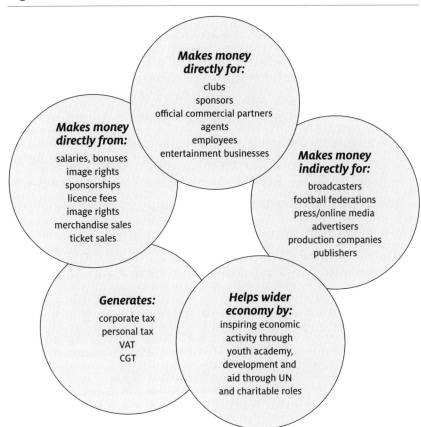

SOURCE Adapted from *Brand It Like Beckham* by Andy Milligan (Marshall Cavendish, 2004)

- makes money indirectly for broadcasters, football federations, press/online media, advertisers, production companies, publishers
- helps the wider economy as it inspires economic activity through the MLS franchise, youth academy, development and aid through UN and charitable roles

Many brands could do a lot worse than learn from him.

What all of these brands have in common – be they a product or a personality, a curator of content or a corporate service – are the essential criteria for being a successful brand:

- First and most fundamentally, they are all trademarks. You simply cannot be a brand in any meaningful sense if you are not a registered trademark. BMW is. Beckham is.

- You need to be in a functioning, growing and competitive market. British Telecom was the name of a state monopoly; BT became a brand in an open deregulated market. Even the Beckhams compete for attention with other celebrities.

- You must have the ability to trade continually. This might sound obvious but it is worth reinforcing. Brands die when they are no longer relevant and therefore people no longer buy them. In 1996, Interbrand placed Kodak in its Top Ten. Where is it now?

But still the myth persists that brands are packaged goods. An advertising executive said recently to us: 'You use the term brand like no one else; for everyone else brand means products they buy on shelves.'

We argued that in fact we use brand like anyone else. Brand is what your name represents in the mind of your customer, your employee and anyone else whose opinion about you counts. And that is true whatever you sell.

Further reading

Andy Milligan, *Brand It Like Beckham*, Marshall Cavendish, 2010

BRANDS ARE JUST ABOUT WHAT HAPPENS ON THE OUTSIDE

In this era of total branding little distinction should be made between employees and customers.

It is a common myth across the business community that brands have a lot to do with what happens on the outside of a business and not very much to do with what goes on inside. This is profoundly wrong. Brands are everything to do with what happens on the inside.

Brands are about much more than appearances

Many people wrongly assume that a brand is just about the logo, the packaging or the advertising and as a consequence are inclined to see the brand solely through the lens of how the brand looks. For these people, brands are the business equivalent of clothing or apparel. If you want your business to be well received (goes the theory) then the best thing you can do is change the way the business looks and smarten up your act. To think this way is to entirely misunderstand what is meant by a brand and, worse, it is closing down a potentially powerful source of competitive advantage.

Great brands tend to spend nearly as much time focusing on their employees as they do on their customers and there is a really good reason for this. Studies have shown time and again that there is a powerful link between motivated and engaged employees and strong commercial outcomes.

Why it pays to focus on the inside

The most celebrated of the models that demonstrate this link was developed at Harvard Business School and it is called 'The Service-Profit Chain'. This model effectively establishes relationships between profitability, customer loyalty and productivity. The links in the chain (which they regard as akin to propositions) work like this:

> Profit and growth are stimulated primarily by customer loyalty. Loyalty is the direct result of customer satisfaction. Satisfaction is largely influenced by the value of services provided to customers. Value is then created by satisfied, loyal and productive employees. Employee satisfaction in turn, results primarily from high quality support services and policies that enable employees to deliver better results to customers.

Figure 7   The link between engaged employees and improved outcomes

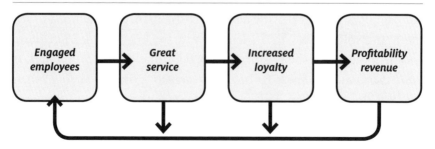

What the academics at Harvard were able to quantify is something that when you think about it makes perfect sense. How your employees feel about where they work has a big influence on how they act, and how they act has a big influence on how customers feel. If you really want to shift your Net Promoter Scores (NPS) then start taking your employees seriously.

The best way to build a brand that customers will love and admire is to start by winning the hearts and minds of your employees. The brands that are celebrated for their distinctiveness and high levels of customer service are generally businesses that see their employees as critical to delivering the brand. Take a look at some of the most successful global brands. It is no coincidence that brands like Apple, Google, Coca-Cola, Facebook, IBM, GE, Disney, Nike and Ikea (to name just a few) are businesses where the brand matters as much on the inside as it does on the outside.

Brand and culture are inextricably linked

The very best brands don't tend to make a distinction between 'brand' and 'culture'; in businesses like Nike and Ikea they are tantamount to the same thing. This is an important point because, in many organizations, different functions tend to operate in their own silos. So brand becomes the responsibility of the marketing department, the human resources team have responsibility for culture and the customer service team lead the attempt to improve the NPS. In brand-led organizations the situation is very different. The business has a clear sense of what it is trying to achieve and as a result the brand is owned by the whole business. Rather than trying to compete with each other, different functions then collaborate to find the ways in which they can manifest the brand both inside and outside the business.

Brands are about the way you do business

In a brand-led business this approach starts at the top. Brands like Apple and Coca-Cola view their brand as the face of their business strategy. There is no arbitrary separation between the 'hard stuff' and the 'soft stuff' – they are seen as inextricably linked. In this type of organization a presentation to investors will typically start off by outlining the brand or organizational purpose, then move to demonstrate how the strategy will help the business achieve that purpose and then demonstrate how the brand will be used to enact that strategy with employees and customers.

As well as a clear and unequivocal statement of their brand intent, these businesses tend to operate in a way that is both tight and loose. They will be very tight on a few brand essentials, ethos and values etc, but looser when it comes to how the brand is executed. This often contrasts with the 'loose and tight' approach, usually in evidence at less enlightened organizations This often-encountered situation is where a business is actually quite loose about what it stands for but incredibly tight and controlling when it comes to every aspect of execution. You know the type: no one inside the organization is really sure what they are trying to achieve but they do know that the greatest sin of all is using the wrong version of the logo!

We have seen the leadership of businesses that profess to be brand-led struggle to even recall their own brand values. In one particular instance a senior leader even admitted that the reason he couldn't recall the values was that there were too many of them to remember. If the senior leadership of a multinational business can't remember their organizational values, either because they are a bit meaningless or there are too many to remember, then how seriously is the brand being taken further down the business?

Brands help protect your business and attract talent

In an era where reputations are hard-fought and easily lost it is vital that employees are clear about the type of behaviour that is not acceptable. Employees need to know what the brand expects of them and how they can escalate issues internally (without fear of reprisal) if they see something illegal, immoral or inappropriate. A clear and understandable set of brand values can help an organization anchor the behaviours it is seeking.

A brand-led business will also typically invest heavily in high-quality recruitment processes and they will spend time inducting their new employees into the business. Emphasis will be placed not just on what the business does, but on why it does it and how it does it. The best brands are not seeking uniformity from their staff: they are seeking to instil the notion of freedom within a framework. It is no coincidence that a candidate seeking employment at Goldman Sachs is likely to be interviewed six or seven times before being asked to join. Or that Pret A Manger give existing store staff the final say on who joins their team. Brand-led businesses know that getting and training the right kind of talent are key to high performance. Such businesses will also seek to ensure that the employee experience is first class and that employees are continually trained and supported such that they can be the very best versions of themselves.

How brands can win hearts and minds

People often mistakenly believe that employees' goodwill can be bought simply by giving out good stuff. No amount of holiday buy-back or free coffee is going to make up for being poorly managed or badly mistreated. Winning hearts and minds is about:

- Establishing a clear and motivating purpose or objective for your brand, clearly articulating the 'why' as well as the 'what' and the 'how'. As we point out in Chapter 11, a brand purpose is not the same as corporate social responsibility (CSR). It is the authentic articulation of what it is that matters most to both your customers and your employees. Premier Inn's purpose is simply to: 'Make our customers feel brilliant.' And this is enacted through a proposition, which aims to give customers: 'A great night's sleep'. No one inside Premier Inn is unclear about what they are trying to achieve

- Developing a brand-led employee experience that taken as a whole demonstrates the value placed on employees. This includes developing a few internal hallmarks that reflect your brand intent, for example ways of feeding back, opportunities to develop new skills, rituals to welcome new joiners. Ultimately, though, the employee experience is defined by the quality of the management. This isn't so much about style (as this can vary enormously) but more about intent, decency and support. Southwest Airlines is globally famous for the quality of its customer service. But at Southwest it is also acknowledged that the customer isn't always right. If a customer makes a dishonest complaint or behaves reprehensibly towards a hardworking employee then Southwest might 'fire' the customer and show support to its employee. This helps to engender employee loyalty.

- Giving sufficient freedom and support to employees so that they are consistently able to act in the best interests of customers. Virgin is a brand often celebrated for the quality of its customer service. Virgin does well not because it necessarily has better training than anyone else but because employees know that Virgin is on the side of the customer and they are prepared and encouraged to go further because they know that is what the brand would expect of them. That's why, as we said in an earlier chapter, Virgin was able to turn a guy stuck in a toilet on one of their trains without any toilet paper into a social media win.

Outstanding customer service comes from an employee instinctively knowing how to respond to a situation and then having the courage to act because they know the brand has their back.

Employees can be powerful ambassadors

Enlightened brands are also obsessed with their customers. They rightly see their staff as both ambassadors for their organization and an important connection point with customers. Even if you don't subscribe to the idea that there is a direct link between how your employees feel and how your business is performing then you must surely see their potential as ambassadors? On the basis that we know how important word of mouth is, we are constantly amazed that many large organizations spend such little time helping to turn their employees into advocates.

Nissan's manufacturing plant does a great job here. Not only does it have a clear brand purpose, a motivated workforce and an ongoing programme of customer and community engagement, but it also runs schemes to allow employees (and their families) to purchase cars at heavily discounted rates. Employees who are both making and owning the vehicles are the very best kind of ambassador. They are demonstrating their confidence in the brand by spending their own money.

Treat the cause of your malaise and not just the symptoms

It's often easy to spot a brand that requires help on the inside. A bit like when you are feeling unwell: the symptoms can often lead you to the cause. How often have you heard things like: 'I am not really sure what the company is trying to achieve' or 'I know we need to change, but I am not quite sure how we intend to do it'. Often business leaders will talk about 'employees not really getting it' or express their frustration at the 'lack of change within the business'. All of these statements are really exposing a failure to engage staff and many of these issues can be addressed by harnessing the power of brand.

When seeking change start on the inside

When it comes to changing your strategy or repositioning your brand, you would do well to first engage with your employees. What hope do you have of delivering a new strategy to customers if employees are unclear about why the organization is changing direction as well as what is now required of them? Brands should apply the same tools and techniques to their internal audiences as they do to their customers. Hearts and minds are rarely won over with a fifteen-minute PowerPoint presentation.

A lot of nonsense is spoken about engagement programmes. In many businesses it is as though a collective amnesia descends the minute the business starts having to engage internally. Employees should be treated just like a more intimate group of customers. It is naive to think that material produced internally (such as videos or presentations) won't finish up being shared on social media. Assume that it will be and then start using that to your advantage.

Accept that, just like your potential customer base, you are unlikely to convert everyone to your cause. Don't waste time trying to play chess with people who ultimately don't want to play chess. Instead focus on the employees who are open to change and target your resources where you know it matters. Communicating any type of change requires employees to first hear about the change, then to understand the change, then to see the change happening and ultimately to believe in the change. Treat your engagement like an ongoing campaign. Use the full suite of appropriate channels, encourage dialogue, and don't hide from the difficult questions. Accept that the process is ongoing.

Why it pays to get it right on the inside

All of this matters because delivering for customers is getting more complex. The most progressive and fast-moving brands are no longer working in silos. The internal structures within organizations are changing to reflect the need to have a single view of the customer and deliver seamless customer service across any type of device or access point anywhere in the world.

Agile teams come together to solve specific issues and then dissolve again once the issue is fixed. Teams are networked and diffuse. The best way of meeting this challenge is to make your brand work as hard for you internally as it does externally. Create a strong purpose and use it to drive meaning and coherence across your organization. Treat your employees as more intimate customers. Recognize the potential of your employees to act as ambassadors. Engage effectively and welcome challenge. Get your employees to share customer problems and harness their expertise to help you solve them.

We live in the age of total branding. It is not possible to divorce or hide what goes on in an organization from what is happening outside. Brands are essentially porous. We know that what happens inside an organization has a direct influence on how a business performs. Motivating and engaging your employees are the best way of improving your customer service and increasing your customer satisfaction. Great brands spend a lot of time engaging and nurturing their employees because they know this is the way to achieve outstanding results and celebrated service – they make sure that their staff know what behaviour is expected of them and how they can individually play their part in the development of the organization.

In this era of total branding little distinction should be made between employees and customers. Both have the potential to be passionate advocates for your brand and both are critical to your success. To get it right on the outside you first have to get it right on the inside.

Further reading

The Service-Profit Chain: https://hbr.org/2008/07/putting-the-service-profit-chain-to-work

THERE IS NO SUCH THING AS BRAND LOYALTY

*Brand loyalty is now hard earned. But brand loyalty
still exists and it still pays.*

For years marketers have obsessed about brand loyalty. They yearn for millions of consumers to buy their brands, only their brands and always their brands. During the 1990s and the early 2000s, the desire for such devotion to their brands made marketers talk in almost religious tones about the adoration in which they wanted their brands to be held. There were whole books exploring this phenomenon, such as Patrick Hanlon's *Primal Branding: Create zealots for your brand, your company and your future*. We have written elsewhere in this book about the quest for 'fandom', for a sense of almost tribal belonging, a shared sense of identity with the brand that brand owners seek. There are a few books about that too, such as *Tribal Marketing, Tribal Branding: An expert guide to the co-creation process* by Brendan Richardson.

Why brands want you to be loyal

The economics of brand loyalty are simple and compelling, which is why marketers search for it. Loyal customers who repeatedly buy your products or services are more profitable than new customers because they no longer have any costs of acquisition associated with them. Furthermore they will do your marketing work for you, recommending or advocating and even sometimes ensuring that other people buy or try your brand. A study by Bain and Company published in the *Harvard Business Review* found that by increasing customer retention rates by 5%, profits could be increased by between 25% and a staggering 95%.

However, in recent years doubts have been cast over the concept of brand loyalty and whether it exists any more. The argument goes that as more and more sectors and segments face greater competition and more commoditization, so pricing drops and factors such as ease and convenience become more important. So how important is brand other than as a simple badge to help you find a product or service?

In addition some brands – such as Amazon, Facebook, Google or YouTube – are virtual monopolies. What is the direct competitor to any of those? So how can there be any meaningful brand loyalty in those categories?

Did brand loyalty ever exist?

Moreover, some brand loyalty is not loyalty but a form of bribery. The loyalty schemes and club cards to which brands want you to sign up use the language of loyalty but the mechanics and principles of rewards. If you buy from us, you'll get discounts or points you can use to buy more from us. That is not really loyalty, is it?

And some loyalty is not loyalty: it's a trap. Banks, telecommunications firms, leasing arrangements with carmakers often tie you into them through contracts. Or they make it so difficult to switch that inertia takes over and you stay with them while regularly berating the standard of their service.

Judging by the amount of switching that is now occurring in those sectors, as government regulators have become even more champions for consumers and insist that companies make it easier to leave them, there's little love toward the brands in evidence.

But there is plenty of evidence that brand loyalty still exists. Moreover this loyalty is genuine loyalty, customers who are really fans of the brand, so much so that they will play a disproportionate role in the development of that brand.

However, that brand loyalty is hard to achieve, probably harder than ever because it requires an enterprise-wide focus on delivering a consistent brand image and experience.

Evidence of the enduring phenomenon of brand loyalty can be found in the use of and results of the Net Promoter Score (NPS). This has become a favourite metric of many organizations to help them predict the levels of security of demand from their customers and also to identify and adjust elements of the brand experience that need fixing.

NPS is a very simple metric that can also be collected simply; those are among the reasons why many companies favour it. Essentially it asks customers to rank on a scale of 1 to 10 or 1 to 5 how satisfied they are with the brand overall or with a specific experience of that brand. By adding up the numbers of people scoring highly (9 or 10, say) and then subtracting those scores which are low (6 and under for example), you arrive at a net score which indicates how prepared generally consumers are to promote you or recommend you to someone else. That is seen as a good proxy for brand loyalty. Repeatedly, research indicates that only people who are scoring you 9 or 10 out of 10 or 4 or 5 out of 5 are genuinely consumers or customers who are so happy with you that they would not leave you and would probably buy more from you. Anything less than that and that customer or consumer is not loyal and is indeed at risk of leaving you for a more attractive proposition.

The popularity of the NPS has become such that unfortunately it is being overused to the point of counter productivity. You may well, as we have, become frustrated by the number of emails or texts you receive asking you to rate how satisfied you were with almost every interaction you have had with a company, often within seconds of having it. The true value of NPS, in our opinion, is in understanding how people think about your brand in its totality, rather than at every single touch point. By bombarding people persistently with desperate requests to 'rate my service' you risk irritating them or, worse, you may get skewed results and also a much less happy customer.

Nevertheless, NPS is a good indication of which brands have loyal customers. In the banking industry, for example, First Direct bank has a consistently high NPS which correlates to other evidence that shows people love and are loyal to that bank, including the number of times that they actually recommend the bank. It is reported that First Direct customers recommend the bank to someone else once every fifteen seconds.

We're still loyal to brands we truly like

Other evidence of brand loyalty is the Meaningful Brands Index. This is a survey conducted by Havas, an international media group, every two years. It asks over 300,000 consumers around the world to rank the brands that they use according to how important they are to them. They have regularly found that consumers have no real loyalty to around 75% of the brands they buy. If those brands were unavailable for any reason or no longer existed, consumers would happily find an alternative. But there are brands which are very important to consumers. These are brands with whom they have such an affinity, a sense of shared or common values, that they are almost indispensable to them in their lives. These are the brands Havas calls the 'meaningful' ones. In the most recent survey, Havas discovered that these meaningful brands produced strong economic benefits to their owners. They outperformed on marketing key performance indicators (KPIs) such as showing a ninefold increase in share of wallet. The businesses that owned them also outperformed the stock market indices by around 206 per cent. The important conclusion that Havas regularly makes in its Meaningful Brands survey is that consumers will have a strong affinity and a desire to repurchase a brand, which does more than provide simple convenience and ease or other kinds of transactional functions. They want an ongoing interaction with a brand that does something special for them and for the world in which they live. These are brands with purpose. Apple, Lego, Harley-Davison and Patagonia are such brands.

Brand loyalty, then, may be harder to achieve now but once earned it is more 'sticky'. Brand loyalty now also manifests itself in different ways than in the past.

Previously, consumers would demonstrate their loyalty by publicly wearing the brand badge as well as with their repeated purchases. There are still people who will wear a brand with pride, including Harley-Davison owners who will happily tattoo the Harley-Davidson logo on to their skin. But more interestingly, loyal customers also want to become involved in the development, improvement and communication of their favourite brands.

Loyal customers now co-create with brand owners

One example of this is Lego and its influential group Adult Friends of Lego, which originally stemmed from a couple of enthusiasts on the internet forming the Lego Users group in 1997. These were adults who were passionate users of the brand. Eventually Lego gave these people the name Adult Friends of Lego or AFOLs. Lego began to tap in to the insights and experiences of these consumers, using basic channels such as email. They discovered that many of these adults were professionals who could give very specific advice on how to make the Lego toys as relevant or true to life as possible. They were, for example, doctors, ambulance workers, fire workers, pilots, even architects. The user group evolved and with the advent of social media and the expansion of digital technology it became an even more popular and creative community. So valuable were they in both product development and brand advocacy that Lego made them Ambassadors and created the Lego Ambassadors programme for them. Listening and working with them, the company understood that its brand was not restricted only to real bricks but could be taken into digital design and moreover across a range of constructive play media, including films. It was in fact the Adult Friends of Lego and the Lego Ambassadors Club which helped to develop the idea of The Lego Movie. This $60 million two-hour advert for the Lego brand has made over $400 million at the box office as well as stimulating new product lines and therefore revenue streams. It was also a critically acclaimed and much loved movie. It was the ultimate example of a fan's fantasy – indeed of a brand manager's fantasy. Brand loyalty was translated into a co-created product and marketing strategy and campaign, which were almost guaranteed to be successful because the people who would consume it created it. In 2014 Lego redeveloped the Lego Ambassadors club into a new type of network community. The Ambassadors have helped drive Lego's growth. In 2016 it sold 75 billion parts and recorded $5.38bn worth of sales.

Loyal customers become great advocates

Another brand which has been built through the repeated behaviour, purchase and communications of its customers is Primark.

This fast-fashion retailer has experienced exponential growth since 2008, with sales rising from around £1.6bn to £7.1bn in little over a decade. Stores have mushroomed across Europe and into America. Primark has invested little in advertising to achieve its brand recognition. Its growth has been driven by its customers who flock through its doors to buy bagfuls of the 'amazing fashion at amazing prices' it stocks and to enjoy the bustling atmosphere and experience of the stores. The products, the stores and the incredible advocacy by its customers online and offline have turbocharged its growth. Shopping at Primark has become something of a social ritual. Meeting friends, chatting online about going, then going to the store and later chatting online about what you have bought has become an almost communal experience of extraordinary importance in its customers' lives.

Just like Starbucks and Metro Bank who we mentioned in Chapter 7, Primark understands that its stores are the best advertisements for its brand. Large, open, glass-fronted buildings, situated on high streets and secondary streets as well as shopping centres, act like living billboards for the brand. The distinctive and sturdy brown paper bags which customers fill with as much fashion items as they can, and which can then be seen carried around towns on buses, through streets or on trains or subways, provide a fantastic advertising space for Primark. The slogan 'amazing fashion, amazing prices' is emblazoned on the side together with a clear message that the bag is recyclable. Customers have also been building the Primark brand through advocacy on social media, in particular through a ritual which has become known as the Primark Haul. Customers, particularly teenage girls, go to Primark and buy a whole selection of fashion items. They then return to their bedrooms, switch on their webcams or smartphone cameras, and record a video of themselves talking about what they have bought, why they have bought it, the price, and how and when they intend to use it. These Primark Haul videos have become so popular that one vlogger called Zoella had over a million followers by 2014. That's a million dedicated members of Primark's target market watching completely unpaid-for advertising and advocacy for the Primark brand. So popular is the brand with its customers that they have developed their own language with regard to how it fits into their lives. Customers like to mix and match Primark clothes with clothes from other usually more expensive fashion brands. This behaviour they call Primani – that is, mixing an item of Primark clothing with an item of Armani clothing in an act of dressing called layering.

Primark does not commission a great deal of television advertising. The expansion of the stores and the buzz that is generated among consumers do all the work for them. The opening of a new Primark store in a town or city is accompanied by a frenzy of expectation. When Primark opened its first store in Paris there was a queue of thousands waiting overnight to get in. When it opened. the rush of customers inside was similar to what you might find at a rock concert.

Primark has built its brand around its core product, its retail experience, a heavy investment in stores on key locations through cities and towns across Europe and now America, and the devoted following of its customers and their online and offline habits. It has also stubbornly refused to become an online retailer. It has experimented with online shopping but the economics of a fast-fashion retail business just do not work in an online channel. Online is great for showcasing the fashions, and for customers to share their photographs and videos via Pinterest, Instagram and YouTube, among others. There is simply not enough profit margin to justify the expensive process of packaging and despatching products. In any case, as Primark understands very well, the *joy* of the brand is in the experience of going to, browsing through and buying in store.

Get as close to your customers as possible

Primark and Lego show you have to earn loyalty. You achieve it by allowing and positively encouraging closeness to your target customers, getting to know them and trusting that they want you to succeed and may have great ideas to help you.

One sector which relies heavily on such 'customer closeness' is the professional services sector. Long-term brand loyalty can be built here through the close attention to building personal relationships. Bear in mind, though, that the trick is to ensure that the loyalty is to the professional services brand, not to the individual consultant, creative or salesperson representing the professional services company.

We believe that businesses that have consumers or customers can learn something from those businesses that have clients. They can learn intimacy or closeness.

In the book *How To Win Friends and Influence Profits*, there is mention of a study of professional services conducted by the Rim Group (Individual Marketing Efforts, Selling Professional Services). The book reported the response to the question: Which of the following marketing tactics has your firm found to be the most effective at generating new revenue? Websites, newsletters, collateral material, bylined articles, speeches and seminars accounted for only 27%. By far the biggest contributor was 'going to visit clients', which received 61%. There was simply no better way to unlock revenue than spending time face to face with clients, having a meaningful dialogue about their needs and requirements, ideally when you have a specific way of helping in mind. And as is often the case, just by being there with them opportunities to help arise. As Woody Allen said: '80 per cent of success is just showing up'. Client loyalty is important for professional services, just as consumer or customer loyalty is for other businesses. There are a number of reasons why. But perhaps the most important is that it is easier to sell new goods and services to clients who are already fans of your brand than it is to sell existing products to new clients. Of course professional services firms must always seek to win new clients to their brand, but even that is best achieved by showing how existing clients have bought old and new services. People are reassured that people like them have liked you enough to buy something from you.

Consumer or customer (service-led) brands should emulate the degree of intimacy and knowledge that the best client-led companies show. They seek to help rather than to sell. And they can only help if they know their clients well enough to understand how they can help. Moreover, the very best of them allow their clients to help co-create and so own the final solution. Just as Lego, intentionally, and Primark, perhaps with a more hands-off approach, have allowed their customers to build their business.

Brand loyalty is now hard-earned. But brand loyalty still exists and it still pays.

CONCLUSION

Branding fascinates people because it is ubiquitous. We are surrounded by brands daily. But it is only a relatively recent phenomenon. It is only in the last thirty years or so that we have begun to appreciate the disciplines of branding and of brand management, the economic value brands generate and the complex ways in which we as consumers interact with them. So it is not surprising that there are many myths about branding, what it does and what it does not do. We hope you have enjoyed our exposition of the myths in this book.

For convenience, here is the full list of myths and a very brief summary of our main arguments against them.

Myth 1: Brands are just a way of charging you more for the same product

People buy brands for more reasons than just the product. There are psychological benefits from buying brands which transcend product features. Ultimately we, the customers, decide what price we are prepared to pay for a brand. Rather than being fooled into parting with more money than we need to, we often actively collude with companies to pay a premium, because we are buying into so much more than just a simple product or service.

Myth 2: Once lost trust can never be rebuilt

The evidence is that if you have a strong brand and a desire to take decisive and restorative action then in most circumstances (given time) trust can often be either fully or at least partially restored. That doesn't mean that brands can rest on their laurels. Many of the high-profile scandals could have proved fatal if they had affected weaker brands with less robust balance sheets. Trust is hard-fought, easily lost and often costly to restore. But it can be restored and rebuilt.

Myth 3: A strong brand can be used to prop up a bad business

In today's marketplace a brand is not seen as separate or distinct from the business it serves. They are in fact integral to each other. Attempts to use brand identity and advertising as a way of hoodwinking your customers into a poor purchase are likely to prove unsustainable and counterproductive. At the same time if you are a good business and you can apply that virtue to a business and brand that are underperforming you are likely to be able to accelerate the growth and value of your business.

Myth 4: Technology is diminishing the power of brands

Brands are powerful because they help to generate demand and create loyalty. Brands work because they are intimately linked to self-expression. Technology has not changed this. Technology is not challenging the power of brands but it is disrupting markets, transforming business and profoundly changing the practice of brand building.

Myth 5: Branding is just about the logo and advertising

A whole chain of experiences that shape perceptions and preferences creates brands. The logo is always fundamental, advertising is often crucially important, but these are not the essential brand builders. Jeff Bezos famously said that 'your brand is what people say about you when you're not in the room'. And what they say about you tends to be the result of what you say and do. For the modern brand builder in a multichannel world in which people are craving authentic and engaging experiences and not just entertaining advertising, remembering to build your brand on everything you say and everything you do is vital.

Myth 6: Brands don't have financial value

Brands create both financial and economic value. They are specific assets which generate a security of income for any business and they can be sold by one business to another, providing cash for the vendor. They create economic value because of what their owners do with their brands: how they invest in them, how they extend them, how they update them and keep them relevant and fit-for-purpose for their consumers.

Myth 7: Differentiation is dead. Distinctiveness matters

It's not that a brand needs to be distinctive rather than different. It needs to be both. But it needs to focus on what will make it genuinely distinctive and keep focused on delivering that consistently. The combination of that plus the constancy of protecting the brand identity that it owns, and which genuinely differentiates it, makes it remarkable.

Myth 8: The customer is always right

The response to this myth is very simple but it is hard to effect. You first have to know who your right customers are, you then have to know what they most value and deliver it to them. Then if the right customer complains because you are not treating them right, they are right to complain. The *right* customer is always right.

Myth 9: You need many decades to build a truly global brand

It now takes much less time to build a genuinely global brand. Tesla has managed to achieve global brand status in just a little less than fifteen years. It is also quite possible that this process will get even faster. Facebook, Uber or Airbnb all are proof that a brand can rise from relative obscurity and within just a handful of years become a global giant.

Myth 10: A brand is 'owned' by the marketing department

For businesses of all types, future success will depend on the ability to organize around the customer, to accept that reputation is earned and not cynically manipulated, to move from a tendency to command and control towards a more open and flexible way of working. To understand that while trademarks and IP can be legally owned by a business or individual, the real power of brands is that they reside in the mind of the customer and that every single action taken on behalf of a customer has the potential to add value and equity. Brands need to be owned by the board, not the marketing department.

Myth 11: Brand purpose is just CSR by another name

A genuine brand purpose is not about traditional corporate and social responsibility. It is the authentic expression and enactment of an organization's primary motivation, the reason why that brand or business exists in the first place, often found in the one thing that matters most to both customers and employees.

Myth 12: Customers are seeking a personal relationship with your brand

Be wary of the idea that the majority of customers are seeking a personal relationship with your brand; most of them are not. Recognize this and you can start to build a more effective brand. Nurture the smaller cohort of customers who are open to a relationship and help them to build a community where customers can talk openly to each other. Use the money you would have spent trying to build relationships with customers who aren't interested to sharpen your offer, build distinctiveness and use insight to stay with and ahead of changing customer needs and motivations.

Myth 13: Branding is subjective. It's all fluff and art with no rigour and science.

There are definitive tools and established rigorous processes for branding. There is also a range of great expertise and effective processes available to support the brand owner. But importantly, none of these should be considered as a replacement for genuine insight and creative thinking. Brands should be built on clear insight; they should be relevant and distinctive, and they should excite and empower the customer. Creating them is hard work and involves a melding of IQ and EQ. There are tools to guide the practitioner and to provide shortcuts but they should never replace the human factor that sits at the heart of every successful brand.

Myth 14: In certain types of business, brands don't really matter

Brands have a part to play in nearly all aspects of a functioning free market economy. They help to drive value, maintain competitive advantage and are highly protectable. Brands help businesses connect with and retain customers. And customers are the lifeblood of any business.

Myth 15: Branding has nothing to do with the customer experience

Brands are everything to do with the customer experience. Although it is easy to think about brands in purely visual terms, a brand is really the unique mix of emotional and rational associations that form as the consequence of all of our interactions with that brand. As customers have grown more sophisticated and experience more highly valued, so brands have sought to build a more distinctive edge to their experience. Technology is helping to accelerate this change, shifting expectations, disrupting established markets and helping brand owners to build new and more compelling experiences. Getting the customer experience right really matters.

Myth 16: Branding is all about the product

A brand is much more than just the product alone. A brand is a composite of hundreds of activities designed to form and occupy a space in the mind of the customer. A brand, much more than any individual product or service, is still the best way of building and protecting long-term competitive advantage.

Myth 17: Creating brand names is easy

Creating a brand name can look easy and sometimes it can be. The small trader or domestic entrepreneur is unlikely to get too vexed by the process and will probably worry about trademark registration much later on. For most other businesses, though, the process of name development needs to be approached more carefully. The process will need to be carefully managed, with prospective names being both checked for legal availability and cultural and linguistic suitability. That is much harder than it sounds.

Myth 18: Brands are just consumer goods

There are brands for services, business-to-business companies, technology companies, charities, sports organizations and, as David Beckham reminds us, brands for celebrities too.

Myth 19: Brands are just about what happens on the outside

In this era of total branding (where every interaction with a customer affects their propensity to like or dislike you), little distinction should be made between employees and customers. Both have the potential to be passionate advocates for your brand and both are critical to your success. To get it right on the outside you first have to get it right on the inside.

Myth 20: There is no such thing as brand loyalty

The nature of brand loyalty has changed. It requires brands to deliver consistently on their promises rather than bribe people through so-called loyalty schemes. But in return customers will become advocates for your brand. Brand loyalty is now hard earned. But brand loyalty still exists and it still pays.

Tell us what you think

As we said in the Introduction, these are the myths we have chosen and the rebuttals of them are very much our opinions. We'd be delighted to hear from you if you have other myths you wish to share or discuss and of course if you disagree with or want to add to our opinions on the twenty myths.

Please visit **www.thisiscaffeine.com/mythsofbranding**

INDEX